"I needed to read this [book] [brings] to the table in *You Ca[n Let It Go]*. [It speaks] truth about how to get free from offense. Get ready for some real help where far too many of us get stuck."

        Lisa Whittle, Bible teacher and bestselling author of *Jesus over Everything*

"Alexandra Hoover is a strong, gracious leader who women need to hear from. She's our gentle and firm friend, reminding us of the kingdom truth that we can let go but also compassionately guiding us through that process. This book is full of wise insight, generous stories, and practical tools to help women live free. It's a must-read!"

        Jess Connolly, pastor, founder of Go + Tell Gals, and author of *Tired of Being Tired* and *Breaking Free from Body Shame*

"This book is raw and real and healing. Holding on to offense can suffocate the life Christ died to give us. There is another way to live, and in this book, Alexandra walks that path with us."

        Sheila Walsh, author and TV host

"This book is the product of great courage. I read Alexandra's story with my heart in my throat, because she has done the difficult work of excavating her pain in order to understand it, heal it, and guide others through the same journey. If you are struggling with bitterness, unforgiveness, or holding a grudge, this book is going to help set you free."

        Sharon Hodde Miller, author of *The Cost of Control*

"Alexandra is not only my coworker but also my friend. I've seen firsthand how the message of this book has shaped her life, her family, and our church. Her wisdom comes from hard-earned experience, and her words carry the weight of real victory. I can't wait for you to experience the freedom and hope she so powerfully offers in these pages."

        Nick Connolly, author and lead pastor at Bright City Church

"Disappointment, betrayal, and relational pain are unavoidable in this life, but they don't have to leave us crushed by offense. Alexandra is truthful but gentle with our hearts as she exposes the trap of offense and its maladaptive impact that often goes unaddressed. If you've been paralyzed by your pain, *You Can Let Go* is an invitation to break free and loosen your grip on offense so you can more tightly cling to Christ."

Dr. Sarita T. Lyons, speaker, Bible teacher, church leader, psychotherapist, and bestselling author

"Alexandra carries a flashlight into the shadows of offense—a topic too often overlooked in faith circles—and leads the way with courage and clarity. Through her storytelling and willingness to go first, she reminds us that healing isn't some distant, impossible destination but a path we can begin walking today. To know Alexandra is to understand that she shows up to these pages as more than an author; she is a grace-filled leader, a trusted friend, and a steady presence who never sways from the opportunity to guide others toward deeper freedom and wholeness."

Hannah Brencher, author of *The Unplugged Hours* and *Fighting Forward*

"*You Can Let Go* is infused with Alexandra Hoover's trademark honesty for those stuck in pain. The hard-won revelations within these pages are both biblical and practical, making freedom feel accessible again for anyone who has lost hope. With this book, Alexandra ensures that no one must drown in the bitter waters of offense. It is both a kind exhortation for the wounded heart and a bold battle cry against the lies that keep us chained to the past."

Faith Eury Cho, pastor and author of *Experiencing Friendship with God*

"Alexandra gives us a road map for how to handle deep hurt and steward our pain in a way that moves us toward becoming better rather than becoming bitter. I'm so grateful she's chosen to use her wounds to help others heal. I pray that God does the same for you as you read this book."

Debra Fileta, LPC, author, speaker, and founder of the Debra Fileta Counselor's Network

"The question isn't *if* you will get hurt or offended. The reality is that you *will* get hurt and offended, so what will you do with all the emotions that come along with that? *You Can Let Go* by Alexandra Hoover is such a helpful guide in processing these emotions, living out of the freedom found in Christ, and not being trapped by the burden of resentment. If you're tired of letting others control your emotional well-being and ready to reclaim your God-given joy, this book will be the catalyst for profound change in how you respond to life's inevitable disappointments."

Joel Muddamalle, PhD, author of *The Hidden Peace*

"In *You Can Let Go*, Alexandra Hoover writes with the kind of wisdom that can come only from someone who's let God meet her in the depths of pain and offense and who's chosen to live in freedom anyway. This book is a balm for anyone who feels stuck in the ache of relational wounds. With spiritual insight and pastoral tenderness, Alexandra gently guides us toward the kind of emotional healing that only Jesus can offer. Every page feels like a sacred invitation to release the past, trust God more fully in the present, and walk unburdened into the future He has for us."

Cassandra Speer, bestselling author, Bible teacher, podcast host, and vice president of Her True Worth

"We often find ourselves drawn to watching videos and following instructions to build and create things that are both beautiful and meaningful to us. But what if we applied that same level of commitment and intention to healing the wounds and deep disappointments in our lives? *You Can Let Go* offers a candid guide with practical steps for moving toward healing. Alexandra's personal stories of pain and struggle serve as a guide to a process that isn't instantaneous but is within reach."

Noemi Chavez, pastor at Revive Church

YOU
CAN
LET
GO

YOU CAN LET GO

Make Peace with Your Past,
Break Free from Offense,
and Move Forward with God

Alexandra Hoover

a division of Baker Publishing Group
Grand Rapids, Michigan

© 2025 by Alexandra Hoover

Published by Baker Books
a division of Baker Publishing Group
Grand Rapids, Michigan
BakerBooks.com

Printed in the United States of America

All rights reserved. No part of this publication may be reproduced, stored in a retrieval system, or transmitted in any form or by any means—for example, electronic, photocopy, recording—without the prior written permission of the publisher. The only exception is brief quotations in printed reviews.

Library of Congress Cataloging-in-Publication Data
Names: Hoover, Alexandra, author.
Title: You can let go : make peace with your past, break free from offense, and move forward with God / Alexandra Hoover.
Description: Grand Rapids, Michigan : Baker Books, a division of Baker Publishing Group, [2025]
Identifiers: LCCN 2025007191 | ISBN 9781540904881 (paperback) | ISBN 9781540905192 (casebound) | ISBN 9781493451142 (ebook)
Subjects: LCSH: Christian life | Change (Psychology)—Religious aspects—Christianity | Peace—Religious aspects—Christianity
Classification: LCC BV4501.3 .H6753 2025 | DDC 248.4—dc23/eng/20250703
LC record available at https://lccn.loc.gov/2025007191

Unless otherwise indicated, Scripture quotations are from the Christian Standard Bible®. Copyright © 2017 by Holman Bible Publishers. Used by permission. Christian Standard Bible® and CSB® are federally registered trademarks of Holman Bible Publishers.

Scripture quotations labeled ESV are from The Holy Bible, English Standard Version® (ESV®). Copyright © 2001 by Crossway, a publishing ministry of Good News Publishers. Used by permission. All rights reserved. ESV Text Edition: 2016

Scripture quotations labeled NASB are from the (NASB®) New American Standard Bible®. Copyright © 1960, 1971, 1977, 1995, 2020 by The Lockman Foundation. Used by permission. All rights reserved. www.lockman.org

Scripture quotations labeled NIV are from the Holy Bible, New International Version®, NIV®. Copyright © 1973, 1978, 1984, 2011 by Biblica, Inc.® Used by permission of Zondervan. All rights reserved worldwide. www.zondervan.com. The "NIV" and "New International Version" are trademarks registered in the United States Patent and Trademark Office by Biblica, Inc.®

Scripture quotations labeled NKJV are from the New King James Version®. Copyright © 1982 by Thomas Nelson. Used by permission. All rights reserved.

Scripture quotations labeled NLT are from the *Holy Bible*, New Living Translation. Copyright © 1996, 2004, 2015 by Tyndale House Foundation. Used by permission of Tyndale House Publishers, Carol Stream, Illinois 60188. All rights reserved.

Scripture quotations labeled TPT are from The Passion Translation®. Copyright © 2017, 2018, 2020 by Passion & Fire Ministries, Inc. Used by permission. ThePassionTranslation.com.

Cover design by Darren Welch

Published in association with The Bindery Agency, TheBinderyAgency.com.

Baker Publishing Group publications use paper produced from sustainable forestry practices and postconsumer waste whenever possible.

25 26 27 28 29 30 31   7 6 5 4 3 2 1

To my mom.
Your tears weren't wasted,
and mine won't be either.

To the heart and mind reading this book.
This is the beginning of the rest of your life.
Stay the course.

To my family.
Each book and Bible study I write is a sacrifice
of your time, a moment slipped away from you,
given to the world. Thank you for your support
and joyful yes. For encouraging me in ways I
never could have imagined.

And to my kids.
I hope you read this in your older age and it helps
you make sense of your offense and hurt, even if
just a little. I love you.

Contents

Make Peace with Your Past

1. The Pain That Shapes Us   15
2. Where Hurt Begins   33
3. The Hidden Trap That Almost Killed Me   45
4. Turn On the Light   67

Break Free from Offense

5. Let the Grace In   93
6. Step into Acceptance   107
7. Take Back Your Identity   125

Move Forward with God

8. Move Beyond Defeat   145
9. Figuring Out Forgiveness   161
10. Leave the Burden Behind   179
11. Your New Beginning   197

Make Peace with Your Past

The Pain That Shapes Us

I've been trying to heal from hurt for what feels like a lifetime.

It was a meeting at work, and I'd prepared for it for weeks. I was ready and excited to share my ideas with a roomful of people whose approval held more power over me than I cared to admit. The stakes were high, and I knew that being heard was about more than just career advancement; it would be validation, a chance to prove I belonged.

I began my presentation with a steady voice, carrying all the weight of my effort and hope. But before I could finish my thought, a coworker—someone known for steering conversations in his direction—interrupted with a dismissive tone. "We've already tried that," he said, finality and irritation in his voice, his words landing like a stone on my chest. This wasn't his first time showing this kind of behavior toward me or others. I rolled back my shoulders and caught my breath.

The silence that followed felt suffocating. I glanced around, seeing the polite, indifferent expressions on everyone's faces, and in that instant, I felt the ground shift beneath me. The meeting carried on, and the conversation turned away from my idea as if it had never mattered. I sat there nodding, pretending the sting hadn't reached me, pretending the dismissal didn't chip away at the confidence I fought so hard to build.

Later, when the office emptied and the echo of my colleagues' voices faded, the weight of that moment settled in. I replayed it over and over, dissecting every word and every pause. That night, when I was back at home, the memory replayed itself, looping in my mind. The hurt wasn't just about the interruption or irritation toward me—the rejection and constant posture of disapproval was something I had gotten used to. It was about feeling small, overlooked, and invisible in a moment when I had longed to be seen. I thought about all the things I could have said, the ways I should have defended myself. Their rejection left a mark, as much as I didn't want it to.

Moments like this have a way of reminding us of the wounds we've left unhealed for far too long. And it did. I sat there in my living room while the kids tried to share their day with me, and I felt the weight of offense overwhelm me. Every other unhealed wound and carried offense in my life showed up. Every memory where I felt unseen, silenced, or dismissed came rushing back, weaving itself into a narrative that whispered, "See? You don't matter. You never have."

The truth is, I wanted to believe my coworker's words didn't matter. I wanted to pretend that the hurt dissolved with each passing moment. Instead, they rooted themselves into the corners of my mind and built a home there.

I feel like this may have been the last offense that did it for me, the one that numbed me to love, to life, to healing. I became more cautious with my words and more guarded with my dreams. I had spent years trying to believe God would fight my battles, but I felt safer when I took matters into my own hands. That wound, ignored and untended, joined others in shaping the way I perceived everything that came after it. I took up offense, and it held me hostage.

Where Has Offense Led You?

Carrying offense has led me only to insecurity, defeat, and anger. Where has offense led you?

The hurt I've been carrying around has left me more:

- resentful
- impatient with others
- critical
- harsh
- callous
- emotionally reactive
- envious

And it's left me less:

- hopeful
- secure
- patient
- forgiving
- soft
- confident

But how offense has left you is not the end.

I'm not here to explain your pain away. I want you to feel seen and deeply loved. I want you to know that Jesus offers a way in and through your wounds. Every ounce of offense you're carrying is safe with Him, even if it doesn't feel that way right now.

Hurt is universal. None of us escape the effects of living in a fallen world. Disappointment, rejection, and unmet expectations are inevitable. Wounds are among the hardest parts of life, second only to grief and death. But they are not the end of our story. They do not define us.

The thing about offense is that it isn't just found in a passing moment. It's a collection of stories our minds and hearts hold on to, a library that catalogs each moment we are misunderstood, overlooked, or deeply hurt. Faces we once trusted become tinged with pain whenever we recall them. Places that once brought joy now carry an ache, a reminder of conversations that should have gone differently. Offense is made up of more than just what was said or done; it is also about what was left undone. The words we wish we had said keep us up at night.

Offense is the quiet mourning of a version of ourselves we wanted to protect—the person who would have stood tall, known better, said the right words, or walked away sooner. But life is rarely that clean. We collect these offenses, replay our responses, and, without realizing it, allow them to shape us. Each unspoken defense, each moment we wish we could rewrite, becomes part of who we are and how we see the world. And we continue to hold on to all of it, even when everything in us wants to let go.

My whole life, I have wanted to pretend that people's words and actions don't hurt me, but they do. I want to be someone who can easily let go of moments, feelings, and experiences. I want to move past the past. But it chases me in the present. I am made of flesh and bones, and each time I've let a wound go untended, it has become part of the framework from which I see my life. A hurt left untended becomes an offense I pick up.

Wounded? I feel it.

Betrayed? I carry it.

Rejected? I live it.

Belittled, overlooked, undervalued? I hide because of it.

Offended? I embody it.

I used to avoid confessing when someone hurt me and downplayed any offense that crept into my heart. Honestly, there are still moments when I resist owning up to it. I get tangled up in the hurt, caught in its trap, and tied to its lies. The offended heart knows what it needs to thrive: pride, resentment, bitterness, insecurity, and an unforgiving spirit. These are the weeds and vines that choke out new life, and they have been my wilderness.

Offense has a way of following you around once you pick it up. It's everywhere you go.

- The comment from your friend that didn't sit well.
- The belittling remark your coworker made.
- The statement from your spouse that cut deeper than ever before.
- The wound you received from the severing of a friendship that couldn't be repaired.
- The unforgettable pain from your childhood.
- The rage you carry, passed down from the hurt others handed you.

- The apology you never received.
- The invite you never got.
- The "I'm sorry, but we decided to go with someone else."
- The silence that followed when you needed someone to speak up.
- The feeling of being unloved or overlooked by the very people you thought were safe.
- The kind of betrayal that doesn't just break your heart—it breaks your trust in people.

I can understand, for the most part, why things happened the way they did for me. I can even process the reasons behind the hurt. But making peace with my pain? Finding true acceptance in it and learning to move forward? That's the challenge. It's as if living unoffendable is an impossible dream, an existence that feels out of reach, especially when the wounds run this deep. I want to be able to experience hurt without letting it define me. And I want to honor my experiences without allowing them to victimize me.

One challenge in facing our hurt is to stop numbing it long enough to actually see it for what it is. But we are terrified of pain, so we medicate it. We numb it by whatever means we can find, whether through distractions, avoidance, or simply shutting down. We are constantly looking for ways to escape the hurt. Defensive, guarded, angry, resentful, bitter, exhausted, suspicious—we wear it all like armor, thinking it will protect us, but in reality, it only makes us more vulnerable.

Here's the hard truth: Medicating pain doesn't heal it. Numbing hurt doesn't remove it. Bitterness won't heal on its own. Anger won't heal the wound; it will only trap us beneath more layers of offense, building up resentment, bitterness, and exhaustion. We often try to explain away our hurt, thinking it's easier to just move on. But this merely masks it, allowing offense to remain, grow, and begin to define us.

Acknowledging the hurt might feel like admitting defeat, as if facing it makes it more real or permanent. We fear that if we look too closely, we might unravel everything we've worked so hard to maintain. But the more we guard our hearts from pain and close ourselves off to healing, the more we will continue confused and defensive. We must be brave enough to face our offense.

Offense, My Copilot

When I was in kindergarten, my mom dressed me in what I now realize was peak nineties fashion: velvet dresses with bows and shoulder pads, the kind you'd see in a JCPenney holiday catalog. But these weren't just for Christmas or Easter—we wore them year-round. In my family, appearances were everything. No one could know how deeply we were hurting. Whatever was happening on the inside, we made sure the outside looked perfect.

But before those dresses and our move to the US, my earliest memories were rooted in Caracas, Venezuela. I can still feel the warmth of the breeze, the kindness of the people, and the vibrancy of the culture. It was a place where I felt a sense of belonging so deep it still lingers. Joy lived there—unshaken, untouched by the storms that would come later. Sometimes I wonder what life might have looked like if we had stayed. Venezuela held my happiest memories, my purest joy.

Everything shifted when we moved back to the US. My parents had been separated, living in different countries, but I missed my dad deeply. I longed for his love—for a chance at family again. My mom said yes to leaving behind the life we knew, even though it terrified her. She made the move with hope in her heart—hope that maybe, just maybe, something could be restored. She wanted more for me. A father. A family. A future we could reclaim. But her sacrifice unraveled quickly. My dad chose himself over us—preferring another woman and, above all, alcohol. The betrayal cut deep. It didn't just hurt; it hollowed. And pain like that doesn't stay contained. It spills into everything. It steals vision, chokes out hope, and leaves you grasping for meaning.

For my mom, the pain became her identity. I saw it in the way it drained the light from her once playful and charismatic spirit. And I learned from her. As a little girl, I fought to protect her and myself, but in doing so, I picked up the same offense she carried. It became my lens, distorting how I saw the world. All I could see was that no one was coming to love me or save me.

My dad's choices rewrote how my mom saw herself—her worth, her value, her security. She gave everything she had to hold us together, but offense is a venom that poisons everything it touches. Her depression became a silent storm that swept through both of us, shaping my life in ways I'm only now beginning to untangle.

That first week back in the US was heavy with tension and unspoken disappointment. Life doesn't wait for you to catch your breath. I started school, and my mom and I became actors, masking our brokenness with tidy exteriors. I remember gripping her hand tightly as we walked down the school halls on that first day. Neither of us knew how to navigate the trauma we were stepping into. We had no support, no resources. We had felt so brave leaving Venezuela, so hopeful that this time would be different. But it wasn't.

My mom regretted the move almost immediately. The weight of what we had left behind, coupled with the pain of what we had returned to, became too much to bear. She blamed everyone—my dad, herself, and even me, questioning why I ever thought coming back to him was the right choice. But I was just a little girl, and I wanted a dad. I couldn't see the truth of what was happening; all I knew was that I longed to be loved by him, to have him there. Her regret felt suffocating, leaving no room for us to feel settled or safe. The pain she carried shaped everything, and I could feel it shaping me too, though I wasn't yet old enough to understand the depth of it.

Offense and hurt have a way of clouding our ability to love and live with empathy, making us the most selfish and prideful versions of ourselves. My mom's bitterness and regret weren't just her personal struggles; they became a filter through which I saw everything. It was hard to love when it felt like we were both drowning in the same weight of pain.

Layers to Healing

There are layers to healing. Sometimes our genesis stories don't look the way we envisioned or would have wanted, and yet God does something only He can do in them and in us. He reaches back into our past to heal our present. There's always a way forward when God invites us into a new life with Him. It's never too late. If we allow it, facing the immense challenges of life can lead us through a deep process of healing. It has the power to unlock strength, peace, and hope we never knew were possible. Ultimately, it can guide us to the place we've always longed for—a place of true acceptance, security, and wholeness.

One of those layers that needed to be healed began to form in the cold hallways of my new school. My mom had dropped me off, and I was scared for a million reasons. I felt my stomach twist and my chest tighten, my body signaling its anxiety and fear. My throat was dry as if it were closing up, and each breath was difficult to draw. At that moment, I thought, *This is my new life.* Despite the unease, I was excited for recess to arrive. I knew just enough English to get by, and I had my kindness—something my mom had gifted me, along with her smile. She had an incredible ability to bring joy and gentleness wherever she went, loving people so deeply. Suffering can either soften the heart or harden it. It hadn't totally taken hers yet.

On that cold, gray fall day, the playground structure loomed before me, the red metal sharp against the chill. I climbed up the bars, eager to go down the slide. But as I reached the top, an overwhelming awareness washed over me: I was wearing a dress. Behind me, a group of girls waited their turn to slide down. They didn't have dresses on.

"Hi!" I said. Despite my embarrassment, I couldn't wait to make new friends. A few girls were kind and waved back. We went down the slide, one by one, until my dress got caught on the side. I scrambled down and clumsily met the mulch on the ground. Brushing myself off, I got up and stood to the side, waiting for the other girls to slide down after me. My heart raced with anticipation. I wanted to ask if they would play with me.

As I think back to that moment, I see a willing, openhearted girl, one who reached out first with hope and bravery. What

I didn't know then, and what I would learn much later, was that this kind of vulnerability, this openness, would one day feel like weakness to me. An invitation for betrayal. The sting of past rejections would try to convince me that guarding my heart was safer and that protecting myself was survival.

Before I knew it, one of the little girls was mocking me. "You don't speak English!" she said. Tears filled my eyes, but I was too embarrassed to cry, so I just stood there. Kids will be kids, but no one warns you how much words shape who you become. I ran to my teacher, hoping for comfort. Instead, she brushed me off and told me to stand by her until recess ended. I didn't fully understand what was happening, only that the feeling was familiar. I had felt this shame before. My mind flashed back to the first time I heard my dad say he didn't want us around anymore—just that week. The shame and sense of being unwanted washed over me. My body tensed, and my defense mechanisms kicked in. I had learned what rejection felt like before that day, and this fresh pain only added to my wounds.

Our origin stories give us a framework through which we view the rest of life. My story began with the grueling reality of my dad's alcoholism and betrayal. I picked up that hurt and met offense early on. I became friends with it. I learned to live offended with people and life, and God.

Living offended happens when we make the choice to live from a place of hurt. And it's a choice not just to live with the hurt but to live with the resentment and bitterness that accompany it.

Functional magnetic resonance imaging (fMRI) studies show that when we experience rejection, there is a physical response in our brains that imitates the reaction of physical trauma to the body. Rejection physically manifests as pain in our bodies. Offense *hurts*. I know this firsthand, and I want us to finally learn to heal from it. I want our hearts to experience a new sense of freedom in Christ, one that breeds forgiveness and compassion for both ourselves and others.

God made us to be people free from the chains and the weight of always living offended. He desires for us to have the confidence to live life as He designed it, with love, patience, kindness, self-control, and joy. Through Jesus, He calls us to live in the security of His love so that no matter what comes our way, we will be like a tree, rooted and firmly planted by streams of living water (Ps. 1:3).

We all have defining moments of pain in our lives. But young or old, we have a choice. We can either live offended or release our grip on bitterness. We can't control whether people hurt us. We will sin and be sinned against. Our ability to let go of offense begins with God, with Him as our compass and guide. Because time alone won't heal our wounds, but time with God will.

In the following chapters, we're going to take a look with God at our hurts and hearts. We're going to reach down into the bags of our lives and empty out even the smallest of unhealed hurt. We will look at the ways we have let our hurt become our offense and learn how to respond to our discomfort and pain from a secure and safe place in Jesus. We'll be free to forgive, free to stop living from the offense, safe enough in Christ to trust that He is Lord over all and He will fight for us. We'll finally begin to live *from* love and not *for* it. This is where we'll find true acceptance and true healing. When we can let go.

You may have picked this book up because your heart is tired of living constantly wounded and offended. Maybe you haven't been betrayed but have been widely disappointed and discouraged by someone you trusted. Or maybe you have been betrayed, and the idea of forgiving that person still feels impossible. Perhaps you're tired of feeling constantly insecure and isolated in your pain. You're stuck in the symptom of offense, and it's crippling you. You're weary, wondering how on earth you'll ever love, trust, or walk in victory again. You're tired of living for the consistent need to be loved by people because that previous wound left you empty—looking for love in all the wrong places. Instead of living securely, you're living resentful and angry. You're waiting for the apology, but it's been years and nothing yet. Maybe you're bitter and can't stand who you've become. You've tried being the bigger person, but turning the other cheek is starting to hurt more than the hurt itself. You won't forgive, but you'll think about it. You won't let go, because being right and justified in your pain feels better than you'd like to admit. You want to believe the best, but every time you do, you're constantly let down.

For me, picking up the offense has felt more justifiable than letting it go. I have become more accustomed to a life of offense than a life of peace and acceptance. I learned how to live offended for most of my life. It may sound dramatic, but it's the truth. Until recently, I didn't know a life without that nagging companion, that terrible copilot, constantly whispering lies about my lack and my inability to be loved.

Offense feeds on my doubts, deepening the cycle of self-criticism and hesitation. In my mind, no one seems safe enough because I'm not sure anyone will ever truly love me. Offense keeps me just far enough away from those I care for that real intimacy feels impossible. It feels too costly. This mindset clouds my judgment, making me question my worth, and anchors me in fear and shame.

When we've been walking too long on the path of offense, it's like stepping through wet cement—fresh, heavy, and clinging to everything. At first, we think we're moving forward, but over time, our feet sink. The longer we stand in it, the harder it is to move. Eventually it hardens around us, and we find ourselves stuck—trapped in the very things we never meant to carry this long.

Friend, we have a choice to make. We can continue to hold on to the hurt and offense we are carrying, despite it breaking our backs, or we can choose freedom. This doesn't mean excusing sinful behavior—ours or theirs—but rather healing from it. We are allowed, along with Jesus in Gethsemane, to ask God to let this cup pass from us while we process the pain to make peace with it. We will walk with God on this journey of learning to let go. We won't deny our pain or minimize the hurt, but rather, we will let the hurt hurt. And as we do, we will notice where we need God most.

Weeds and Vines

What resonates with you as you read this is important. The Spirit reveals the things that need His touch and our attention. We can't outrun hurt, but with God, we can prepare ourselves for the inevitability of offense. We can understand, grow from, and even be freed from its symptoms. Living offended is a choice, and we have the power to let it trap us or to free ourselves from it.

When I first began thinking about this idea of letting go, I couldn't help but picture vines. Despite my collection of houseplants and trips to the garden section at Home Depot, I am no gardener. When my oldest daughter was around five years old, she was obsessed with having flowers in our backyard. She wanted a planter, so naturally, I didn't take the easy route. I didn't just buy one off Amazon. Instead, I looked up "DIY planters" on Pinterest, found the most straightforward plan, and built my girl her planter. A few weeks later, we purchased and planted the easiest flowers to keep alive. We were thrilled to see the first sprouts emerge, but a few months later, we noticed some unexpected visitors—weeds. We figured our feathered friends must have carried seeds from their travels, giving the weeds a new home to grow. At first, some of the weeds seemed pretty, but they quickly took over the planter. They choked out the flowers, leaving little room for anything else to thrive.

When the COVID pandemic hit, like everyone else, we had to find new ways to fill our days. That was when I decided to become a "gardener" again—for all of five months. You can laugh at me. This time, though, I was prepared for the weeds. I knew how to protect our planters from being overtaken. I covered the potting mix with a layer of mulch, used weed barrier fabric and pre-weed killer, and even tried some home remedies like salt and vinegar (though I still don't fully understand how those work). Armed with these tools, I hoped for a better outcome.

But it got me thinking: How do we move forward when our feet are tangled in the weeds of offense? How do we love again when our hearts have grown cold with self-protection? How do we step into lives of abundance when the things that define, defile, and deplete us have such power? How do we rewrite our story to one of freedom when defeat keeps replaying in our minds like a song on a loop?

Unhealed hurt grows like weeds that pop up unwanted in our planter boxes, in a hurry to make sense of what's happened.

And when it doesn't know where to go or what to do, the enemy of our souls does. He's ready to show us a way out of hurt every time, and it's never helpful or good.

The hurt grows and creates a habitable ecosystem in us, and then we notice that breathing through the pain has become almost unbearable, taking the breath out of our lungs and our love. Life begins to seem less and less hopeful, and we begin to demonize everything and everyone. No one is safe. *We will never be hurt like this again.*

It's interesting how vines grow at the same speed as weeds. That was the other picture I got when I began thinking about the power of offense in our lives. Vines compete with trees for sunlight, water, nutrients, air, and space. They want to grow and they will, no matter the cost, choking out the branches and even killing the trees. They grow aggressively, with one goal: to take what they need. Once a vine gets itself around something, pulling it off can be a tedious and exhausting experience.

Most of us have spent our whole lives trying to pull the vines of hurt and offense off our hearts and souls, to no avail. And no matter how hard we try to forgive, grow, move on, walk in confidence, be secure, and find joy and life again, we end back up where we started. It's like we made a bad deal and can't escape it.

If we can't pull the vines out of tall trees or other structures, we're told to concentrate on killing or removing the roots. It's the only sure way we'll get rid of the vines. This goes for weeds too. Pull them up.

When our hurt overgrows like weeds and becomes an offense we've picked up, it paints our lives in gray and tries to take every bit of the color out of it. It touches every good thing in its path and wraps itself around whatever it can find.

Sometimes the wound is so complicated, nuanced, and layered that we don't know where to start. How do we pull the root from something so delicate and intertwined without causing mass destruction?

As I write this, I feel the tension of how complicated and tangled hurt is in my own life. I want to forgive. I want to overlook the offense. I want to look at the people who hurt me and tell them how long it's taken to get over the words they spoke at me and over me. I want to go back six years and address a conversation I should have spoken up about. I long to reconcile with God just how disappointed I am with the amount of loss my family has experienced in the last five years, how much I miss the days when life wasn't so full of grief, and how I can't remember a season of my life without disappointment. I've tried to overlook offense through my best efforts. I stare at it just long enough to deal with the initial wave of discomfort, then find a way to live with it, then push it out of sight. I tell myself I've buried it deep enough, but it's only an illusion.

The trap of offense creates fertile ground for resentment, bitterness, and mistrust to take root—a toxic playground we often find ourselves stuck in. These emotions don't just linger; they multiply, feeding on unresolved hurt and unforgiven wrongs. Over time, they grow into walls that foster division, isolation, and a cycle of pain that feels impossible to break. Resentment and bitterness, born from wounds left untreated, lead to offense and anchor us in it, making freedom feel like a distant hope.

Wounds don't just happen, and they don't just disappear either. It's tough to move on from how someone treated us or to forget the ache their words left behind. We replay the hurt over and over, and it starts to shape the way we see everything. The fear of future pain keeps us stuck in the past, unsure of how to let go of the words, the moments, or the people that hurt us. And unless we're prepared for it, those words and actions can become our identity—they start to define us.

The longer we carry offense, the more it shapes us, making it harder to see the life we've been called to—one of abundance, love, and release. The hurt hurts, but healing can also be part of our story.

Where Hurt Begins

It was 1997. My mom picked me up from school, and we headed back home. I could barely see above the dashboard when we pulled up to the house, but I could see a car in the driveway and clothes scattered across the yard. My mom let out a deep sigh, and the car felt colder. The silence was so heavy. The air around us shifted—I felt it in my chest.

Sitting in the back seat, I waited. I knew something wasn't right. I asked my mom, "Who's that woman?" She didn't answer. That's when I noticed a little boy—we looked around the same age—standing by the screened front door, with black hair, pale skin, and a skinny frame. I'd never seen him before. I stared at him, my heart pounding, waiting for something, anything, to make sense.

Finally, my mom spoke quietly, "That's your brother."

Before I could process her words, the silence shattered. She got out of the car. Screams erupted from inside the house, and my world went dark. All I could hear was the sound of my own breathing, which was both too loud and too fast. I stepped out of the car, still unsure of what was happening, as the noise inside the house swelled and swallowed everything else. I had no way of knowing what lay ahead. I only knew the anger burning inside me toward my dad. It was just another offense to add to the long list of hurts he had already handed me. The weight of it all felt too heavy to bear, and yet there I was, standing in the middle, caught between a past I couldn't escape and a future I didn't know how to face.

I've stayed in that same place for a long time.

Offense doesn't just knock on the door and leave; it moves in. It settles itself at the dinner table—uninvited but insistent. It teaches us the anger it needs to breathe, the sadness it requires to survive. Its legs—bitterness and resentment—carry it from room to room, and it makes itself at home in every corner of our hearts.

The trick is in its disguise: Offense convinces us it deserves a seat, posing as righteousness and restitution while quietly poisoning the atmosphere. We want to get even. We want someone to acknowledge the pain. Deep down, we're longing to be seen—to have someone recognize how much it hurt.

But when we allow offense to become our guiding compass, we're shaking hands with the devil. It's like saying, "Yes, I'd like to live angry, defeated, prideful, bitter, insecure, resentful, and envious, thank you." But making friends with our hurt isn't the solution. Instead, we're invited to feel those emotions and align them with a truth far more steady and redemptive than anything we've experienced. This is the path of letting go with God.

I Can't Forget

I wanted to play catch with my dad. I always dreamed of living out the moments I saw on the TV shows I watched. My afternoons were filled with *Boy Meets World*, *The Cosby Show*, and *The Wonder Years*. Sitting on the soft off-white carpet in my bedroom, I watched these shows and got my first glimpse of what a "healthy" family was supposed to look like. I couldn't help but wonder if that could ever be my family.

It was a sunny Saturday, and Dad was home early from work. Maybe today was the day we would finally play catch. My mom and I lived with him for only about two years, and those years were chaotic—borderline hellish, really—but I still held on to some version of hope. I rushed to my room, grabbed a tennis ball, and gathered the courage to ask Dad if he would play with me. I was so nervous. His response was tired, angry, and filled with a sadness I couldn't fully understand: "No, not today. Go make me a drink, please." His love for alcohol always took priority over everything and everyone. I knew that, but I held out hope that perhaps I was different.

I haven't been able to forget the wounds my dad inflicted, and now I realize that I don't think I'm supposed to. If anything, the more I heal, the more I see how deeply the offense hurts, how those words and rejection became my identity, and how his inability to love through his own offense and pain hurt me and so many others. The more honest I get about what hurts and allow myself to grieve it, the more I notice how much I need God and the grace found on the cross.

As I've tried to make sense of that hurt, I've found myself tossing and turning, asking the same questions: Why does rejection have such a hold on me? How do I release the constant need to be loved and accepted? How do I move past such deep rejection and the sting of my dad's words?

The truth is, we carry offense well and hide it until we can't. And then suddenly it comes spilling out on those around us. We join the cycle of hurt people hurting people.

When I finally let Jesus sit with me at the table of my heart, He invited me to look at each hurt that had trapped me in a state of offense. He wasn't afraid of the heaviness I brought with me, or the confusion and chaos that swirled around me. He didn't push away when He saw my sin and the ways others had sinned against me. If anything, He was deeply grieved by them and moved in with compassion to heal and offer living water, quenching my dry and desolate soul.

God understands how deeply betrayal and offense can wound us, and we see that in the words of David, a man who knew this kind of heartbreak firsthand. In Psalm 55, he writes, "If an enemy were insulting me, I could endure it; if a foe were rising against me, I could hide. But it is you, a man like myself, my companion, my close friend, with whom I once enjoyed sweet fellowship at the house of God, as we walked about among the worshipers" (vv. 12–14 NIV).

It wasn't just the betrayal that hurt—it was who it came from. That's the kind of offense that lingers. But David didn't carry his pain alone. A few verses later, we hear his cry and his confidence in God's care: "Cast your cares on the LORD and he will sustain you; he will never let the righteous be shaken" (v. 22 NIV). God didn't just witness David's pain; He held it. And He does the same for us.

It was incredibly painful but necessary to let myself see, know, admit, and heal from all the offense I had been carrying. It required admitting that the people who should have protected and loved me the most were the ones who hurt me the most, and I spent years feeling resentful and angry. I realize these were people who wanted to love me but, burdened by their own offense and pain, didn't know how. They never learned to love people through their hurt and pain. Of course, there were those who intentionally inflicted wounds that left me in unspeakable pain. In these cases, there is no explaining away the hurt, and forgetting it is impossible.

With every fiber of my being, I believe that God offers us a way back to healing and wholeness in Him. We can make peace with the pain. We can let go of each small hurt and towering offense that has become the soundtrack of our lives. When hurt turns into lifelong offense, it can keep us from receiving the new and living invitation God offers (Heb. 10:19–20). I didn't know there was another way, but there is.

When we don't know how to let go, we go where the hurt takes us. Our offense steers the ship. But there's an answer, and it is the gift of letting go.

How God Feels About Our Pain

Establishing a clear vision of how God feels about your pain and hurt is an important place to start on this healing journey. To know that Jesus will sit with you as you read this book, peel back the layered relationships and nuances, and grieve what was and what couldn't be, is where we must begin. We will look to Jesus' life and His profound experience with hurt and pain as our guide. But for now, I'd like to start with these simple yet foundational truths as our compass for this journey.

> God knows, and He sees. He saw it. He sees you, He knows you, and He loves you. This is important to hold on to.
>
> He cared then, and He cares now.
>
> He isn't annoyed or repelled by the offense in you, even toward Him.
>
> He saw every moment when you were a child unable to protect yourself, and he wept over the pain it caused you.
>
> It's not supposed to be this way.
>
> Jesus is the answer to our healing and wholeness.
>
> He saw the rejection from those who should have loved you and handled you with care.
>
> He hates the sins that hurt you.
>
> He was with you when they betrayed you, and He wept over your despair.
>
> He was grieved at how alone and isolated you felt.
>
> He has never left your side.
>
> He isn't in a hurry to fix you but is eager to heal you.

What if it's true that God can take our offense and finally free us? What if there is a life where betrayal, rejection, disappointment, regret, insecurity, resentment, bitterness, envy, and strife no longer define us? What if there is a life on the other side of our hurt?

Most of us have experienced that moment where we look up and wonder, "How did I get here?" This can be our new beginning. It is when our hearts and minds realize there is another way forward that we receive our wake-up call for a new beginning.

I love this truth, and hold it close, that we can begin again with God.

Where Our Offense Takes Us

I've yet to experience any good fruit from carrying offense or allowing my hurt to lead me. The truth is, we're all being led by something, and offense is one of the enemy's favorite guides. If he can get us to follow our pain, we'll stay stuck in it. We'll live from our wounds instead of from healing, reacting instead of rejoicing. And when offense leads, it blinds us to the new mercies God gives us daily.

It's like walking with a broken compass. Earth's magnetic field is designed to help a compass point north—to give direction, to offer clarity when we're disoriented. But even a compass can be thrown off. Exposure to heavy metals or interference from the sun can cause the needle to sway, making it impossible for us to find true north.

That's what offense does to our hearts. It disrupts our inner compass. Instead of being pointed toward the steady truth of God's love and redemption, our thoughts start spinning—pulled by pain, swayed by suspicion, guided by fear. And if we're not careful, we'll follow that broken compass further into isolation, convinced we're right, but deeply lost.

Our true north in the middle of our pain is God's love and grace for us. Yet when pain is left to simmer and idle without being processed, our ability to discern our true north grows weaker over time. Offense disorients us, throwing us off course. Unhealed wounds and unprocessed emotions distort the compass of our souls. Jesus says, "Come to Me," but we often go the other way, pulling ourselves further from grace and deeper into offense. Our souls, disoriented and confused, need to be pulled out of the dark pit of bitterness and pain. The healing we so desperately seek, the wounds we try to mend on our own, can only be truly mended in the hands of a Savior who knows pain even more intimately than we do.

The compass of our souls needs to be recalibrated, not by our own efforts but by turning to the One who guides us gently back to Himself, our true north. It is only in His hands that we can find the healing that reorients us, leading us out of the fog of offense and back into the light of His grace.

Offense in the Garden

In the beginning, God created a world free of hurt and offense. He created Adam and Eve to love Him and be loved by Him. He gave them everything: His presence, power, provision, and purpose. His love created a world for them to rule over in peace. Then sin entered the world, and it wasn't first through the hurt they inflicted on one another but through disobedience to and rejection of God's commands. They chose to prioritize their own desires over God's will. In doing so, they became the bearers of their own pain, captivated by what they allowed to take His place: mere shadows of true fulfillment. Led by pride, they willingly followed its path. And where there is pride, there will always be offense.

What came next was a broken world with a human race desperately looking for security and love. We hurt God and ourselves, yet God offered a way forward. He knows that in this dark and desperate world, learning to heal from hurt and offense is essential for living life abundantly. Through Jesus, He offers a way to make things right. From the beginning of creation to the cross and beyond, God knew what we would need in order to heal and love again. Unlike people, who often remain trapped and immobilized by offense, God responded with sacrificial love. He sent His Son to bear the weight of our sin and brokenness, and Jesus offered His life as a ransom so we could find freedom and forgiveness. Through His death and resurrection, He paved the way forward, giving us hope and the power to be made whole.

In Genesis 3:1–6, the serpent presents a question and tempts Eve:

> He said to the woman, "Did God really say, 'You can't eat from any tree in the garden'?"
> The woman said to the serpent, "We may eat the fruit from the trees in the garden. But about the fruit of the tree in the middle of the garden, God said, 'You must not eat it or touch it, or you will die.'"
> "No! You will certainly not die," the serpent said to the woman. "In fact, God knows that when you eat it your eyes will be opened and you will be like God, knowing good and evil." The woman saw that the tree was good for food and delightful to look at, and that it was desirable for obtaining wisdom. So she took some of its fruit and ate it; she also gave some to her husband, who was with her, and he ate it.

There was internal conflict before the physical act. God had given clear direction: If you eat from this tree, you will certainly die (Gen. 2:16–17). The mind is where every battle begins. Had Eve already been entertaining the idea that God might lie? What ultimately fractured her and Adam's relationship with God wasn't Satan's bait but their choice to bite—their choice to believe there was something better outside of God's perfect design. They took the bait and, in so doing, took up offense with God.

Their eyes were opened. Paradise was shattered. They could now fully see the world of hurt. Misery loves company; it loves to wrap people in a narrative that brings defeat and destruction. When we have no end in sight, no vision or hope for our lives other than selfish ambition and death, and no foundation to stand on other than a withered soul, finding solace and security in the familiar feeling of hurt becomes an overwhelming temptation.

I've always wondered if Eve questioned God's faithfulness. We can't know for sure what went through her mind, but I know I would have been offended had Satan tempted me with a similar lie. *God doesn't have my best interests at heart? Why is He withholding? Why won't He tell the truth? If God is keeping something from us, is His character all that good, anyway?*

The unanswered prayers and pain beg us to find relief, and explaining our pain away won't do it anymore. Friend, it is good to take our anger and doubt to God. There is intimacy and relationship there. God knows our most profound questions, our wounds, our dreams, and the many anxieties of our minds and souls. Our struggle to believe this arises when we assume a position of defense with God and view Him as the enemy instead of as the lover of our souls. What a trap we fall into when we distrust the God of grace and abundance and instead choose to follow a path that leads to pain and brokenness.

Now What?

I remember the first time I felt the sting of rejection. The hurt hindered me, paralyzing my purpose and pausing my growth, and it eventually became a way of life. I was living offended by the hurt of it all.

There is an epidemic of offense in our souls. We are defensive, blinded by our fear and pride, unwilling to open ourselves up to others who might hurt us, and fearful even to try. At the smallest offense, we are sent back to the first time we were ever hurt. We appear stoic while secretly harboring resentment, and it stunts our healing and growth. So many of us are silently pulling away while still attending Sunday services and small groups. We might seem fine on the outside, but inwardly we are carrying deep wounds into every relationship. We are stuck, tangled in the weeds of our pain. This is what offense does.

Learning to let go of hurt will require you to deal with the wrongs you have been carrying around for ages, which means addressing that initial hurt. What did you do with it? Did you tuck it away? How you learned to deal with that hurt is most likely the tool you're using today to move on. But it takes more than a willingness to move on, more than the courage you've bottled up in your jar of tears. It will take a power that you and I don't hold, but our friend Jesus *does*.

Hurt hurts because it simply wasn't supposed to be this way. Our Jesus knows every hurt we experience on this side of heaven, and He gave His life as a living sacrifice to be the balm for the bruises we have collected.

You don't have to wonder if God sees you. He does. You are not alone in this journey, and who knows? What is yet to come may just be the most beautiful part of your story.

3

The Hidden Trap That Almost Killed Me

My husband and I grew up in very different worlds. I was raised mostly by a single mom who was in and out of a relationship with my biological dad. She eventually married my stepdad, but that relationship ended in a hard divorce when I was seventeen. I knew more about horoscopes, angel numbers, and Saturday mass than anything else. Jesus was a distant thought.

The only time I remember being deeply moved by the idea of Jesus is when I glanced over at the paintings of His beaten and bloody face hanging on the walls of the Catholic church. The crosses depicted a body torn apart and worn down, a life given for the very people who mocked and murdered him. I was always moved when I noticed the pain Jesus endured. I knew it meant something. There was a cost, although I didn't know exactly what.

My husband, Mario, grew up in the kind of home I envied most of my life: steady, loving, with a family who was present. They were not perfect by any means, but they had willing hearts and a desire to honor and love God. There was a stark contrast between our lives as we were growing up, and I carried a deep shame over what my childhood looked like. I had survived years and years of trauma, while Mario experienced a fraction of the chaos I carried. I did not wish to compare our pain, as though we were competing in some sort of suffering Olympics, but my pain and past were a reality I had to wrestle with in our marriage.

Maybe the offense you carry has been your constant companion, woven into your story for as long as you can remember. Or perhaps, like Mario, you had a relatively good childhood, and the weight of suffering came later in life—unexpected and new. The pain feels raw. The offense is fresh. You might be reading this book to prepare for future struggles, or maybe you're here because you're ready to move forward from where you are right now. Either way, while our stories differ and the paths to offense vary, the solution remains the same: We must learn to let go, with God's help. I had to learn to let go, to walk the path of laying things down, even at the cost of my pride, my sense of control, and the safety of staying in my pain.

Mario and I have been in a season of our marriage and life that has been full of loss. We have lost people we love and moved to a different state, leaving everything we knew behind. It feels like we kicked up the dust and are now letting God sift through different layers of our lives, allowing Him to tend to our individual and shared pain. We have picked up so much offense along the way. But God, in His grace, walks us gently and generously through our pain, in season and in

His time. He knows when to allow the dust to settle or rise up. When we say yes to Him, the holy work of restoration and reconciliation can finally begin. And when we allow God to heal our wounds, we will begin to see restoration happening all around us, even if it looks different than we thought it would.

One night before bed, I struck up a conversation with Mario about the tension we had been feeling. "I am feeling incredibly resentful toward you and God. I just want to unpack it."

Mario said something that felt like a jab, although it wasn't intended that way. "You deal with pain differently than I do."

My guard immediately went up.

Mario continued, "I'm just figuring out how to process my pain. You've picked up ways to press into it your whole life."

He was right. I'm a veteran in pain and offense, having learned along the way how to move through most of it. If I hadn't, my soul would have been crushed. I had to learn how to survive.

Mario's experience with offense and pain has been different. While his home life may have been steadier and calmer than mine, his deepest wounds have come from within the church. His betrayal came from watching those who professed their love for God choose to love themselves more. Because the source of his pain is different from mine, it has taken time for me to recognize his woundings as true suffering.

For him, it wasn't God who was in question but the integrity of the church and its people. He felt deeply let down and disappointed, unsure of how to trust or love again. His heart had grown distant from the people he once cared for. Sometimes we don't realize how we've responded to offense until we confront it. In our attempts to comfort ourselves, we often end up comforting our offense instead. While trying to console our souls, we inadvertently coddle the hurt.

Neither of us expected to fall into the snare of offense, but it will tempt all of us eventually. This is why we need to learn to deal with our hurt before it deals with us, before it becomes the compass for our souls, like it did for Mario and it did for me for so much of my life. This bitter compass only enables us to operate from a lack of empathy and humility, forgetting that we are in need of God's abundant grace. The trap of offense tempts us to sentence others with a level of severity we would never want for ourselves. It shifts our focus from healing and growth to bitterness and isolation, drawing us further from the love and empathy we're called to embody.

This season of hurt left Mario and me deeply wounded, questioning where we'd gone wrong. But in His mercy, God revealed two hearts that were fragile, guarded, and afraid to trust or forgive. It was through this season that we realized healing wasn't something we could manage alone. We needed God to mend what was broken.

Healing the Layers

You might be thinking, *Alexandra, that sounds great, but I've tried to let go and I just can't.* I want you to know that living free from offense is possible, but it's not about trying harder—it's about surrendering deeper. With God's grace as our guide and protector, we can begin to loosen our grip on the hurt we've held so tightly.

This is something I wish we could talk about more—how letting go isn't a single moment; it's a lifelong journey. It's a constant choice to release the hurt to God, to begin to see the ways in which we've been hurt so we can heal. It takes patience, grace, and a willingness to invite God into the mess. Healing happens in layers, and every step forward, however small, brings us closer to freedom. When we let God into our pain, when we stop running from it and start trusting Him with it, the process of release and renewal begins.

Healing is rarely simple. It's uncomfortable and unpredictable, and it often forces us to face what we'd rather avoid. But in the raw, unfiltered moments of honesty and vulnerability, God's grace meets us. And it's there in His presence that we find the strength to let go, the courage to heal, and the hope to move forward, one step at a time.

I want to be honest with you—up front, right now—that letting go of offense isn't something I have mastered. None of us will. Rather, it is a path we choose to take with God, bit by bit, as we release the ways we have been controlled by offense and hurt. A journey where we learn to let God heal our hurt instead of living offended by it, and we allow Him to shape us into people who are both strong and soft—strong enough to stand in His truth and love yet soft enough to extend grace and forgiveness to others. I don't know a single person who hasn't wrestled incessantly with the need to hold on when they wanted to let go. We remain in discomfort because we are familiar with our pain, and the idea of choosing to let go of offense scares us as we face a future we may not be ready for and a reality we wish we didn't have.

Every day, I see more clearly the way forward with God in my hurt—how to live surrendered, secure, loved, and unoffendable. And I can tell you this: Though the road is long, I have become a less offendable woman, willing to let God sift so I can soar. I'm learning, however imperfectly, to live loved, to trust, to walk with people, and to serve them without holding back.

One thing we all have in common is pain. In some ways, it's even more universal than love—everyone experiences it. Deep down, we know pain wasn't part of the original plan. All it takes is a look at the story of the garden of Eden to see that pain wasn't God's design or dream for humanity. It's natural for us to avoid pain, to flinch when we see someone else hurting, and to feel a sense of connection with others who are suffering. Pain unites us, even when it's the very thing we long to escape.

As we journey toward healing, we have to confront a hard truth: Healing requires honesty. We can't move forward until we're willing to face the depth of our hurt and acknowledge the ways we've allowed offense to take root in our lives. This means standing face-to-face with the pain—examining the wounds of betrayal, disappointment, and bitterness—and choosing to invite God into those broken places. It's not easy, and it will cost us something. But in that mirror, as we see ourselves through His eyes, we can begin to declare, "I am loved. I am valued. I am ready to live again." Healing may feel impossible in our own strength, but it's not in God's.

Inside Out

It was a rainy Monday night, and my daughter Sophia had asked to watch one of our favorite movies, *Inside Out*. Without giving the movie away too much, I'll summarize the gist of it. Five animated emotions—Joy, Sadness, Anger, Disgust, and Fear—offer helpful insight for kids (and even for adults) when it comes to recognizing our emotions and the power they have in our lives. I hadn't watched the movie in over two years, so I had forgotten much of the storyline. I am a deep feeler, which means I cry just about every time I see something that moves me. Consequently, I find the animated version of Sadness, our little blue friend in the film, irritating. She is always in Joy's way, keeping Riley, the main character, from the simple happiness she has always known. Joy wants Riley's happiness protected at all costs, which means no other emotion can even access her.

But Sophia loved the character of Sadness. And maybe understood her more than I did.

I resented Sadness, maybe because I felt like she was in the way of my joy too. I resented not only Sadness but the hurt that first invited her inside my heart: the disappointment, the letdown, the grief, and the betrayal. Sadness was soft and open, not eager to wish her pain away. If anything, she was able to offer a more holistic perspective on Riley's life. A core memory of Riley's could hold a vast range of emotions, including sadness and joy.

Toward the end of the movie I finally began to see that one of the main takeaways, at least for me, was that sadness can be a pathway to empathy. Sadness made room for those around her to feel their hurt in order to take a step forward. As Riley let herself experience sadness, her core memories changed from yellow, the color of joy, to a beautiful hue of blue and yellow, like the perfect sunrise. Joy didn't have to protect Riley from Sadness after all. She needed to make room for her.

I know it's terrifying to look directly at the offense we are carrying and to peel back the layers. What will come from it? Will we have to forgive the person who wounded us? Will we have to look at our own shortcomings too? Will we have to grieve the moments we can't bring back or take back? I've noticed that in my own life, I have been more afraid of healing than of staying in the hurt. The pursuit of joy, or counterfeit versions of it, keeps me stuck in a cycle of feeling rejected, abandoned, and disappointed.

It is brave work to walk into new seasons of change and let go of what we've known and grown accustomed to. In each season, our yes and simple obedience to God unlock the door to the next step in our journey. Some seasons will feel barren, cold, and confusing, requiring more pruning of ourselves, while other seasons will feel light and free and bold. God is working in all of them for our healing and growth, even when it hurts.

Where do we begin? I think for me, healing began when I was willing to recognize and process the emotions that were holding me hostage. Picture this: A close friend makes a hurtful comment, leaving you feeling betrayed. Acknowledging the pain means admitting to yourself that it stings, and not brushing it off. You might talk to your friend for clarity, but even if there's no resolution, you choose to release the hurt instead of letting it define you. You let it go, give it to God, and move forward with peace.

A healing heart is one that lets God see the wounds we've been hiding. This is on the other side of holding on to our offense.

Carrying Offense

Hurt happens to us, but offense is something we pick up. And God wants to heal both. He desires to go deep and get to the root of our wounds because He knows how much they shape us. From a Christian perspective, hurt and offense are reminders of the world's fallen nature. The Bible makes it clear that humans are flawed and will inevitably hurt and offend one another. Romans 3:23 tells us, "For all have sinned and fall short of the glory of God." This verse reminds us that every single person—without exception—has fallen short of God's perfect standard. It's an acknowledgment of the universal nature of human imperfection and our propensity to make mistakes.

In Matthew 18:7, Jesus says, "Woe to the world because of the things that cause people to stumble! Such things must come, but woe to the person through whom they come!" (NIV). Here, Jesus is honest about the reality that offenses and stumbling blocks will come. He knows the world is filled with situations and people that can cause hurt. Even Jesus Himself experienced deep hurt and betrayal during His time on earth, showing us that no one is immune.

Understanding the difference between trauma, hurt, and offense is also important. Trauma is deep and often stems from significant and prolonged pain or distress—it alters how we see ourselves and the world around us. Hurt, on the other hand, is the pain we feel when we're wounded by others, whether intentionally or not. And then there's offense: a response we choose.

Having unhealed wounds and holding on to offense can create lasting emotional and psychological burdens. These burdens shape how we trust others, our sense of security, and our overall well-being. This has all been true for me—every bit of it. When we start to recognize how our patterns turn into behaviors, we can begin to identify what may be at the root of it all. We can learn to spot the difference between trauma, hurt, and offense, and we can choose not to pick up offense.

God's grace meets us in these places, helping us to process hurt without letting it fester into offense. His grace invites us to trust Him with our healing, reminding us that He is both our shield and our gentle guide. May we release what was never ours to carry. May we allow God to make beautiful what's been broken.

When Offense Runs Deep

I once felt deeply hurt when a woman I knew—someone I wasn't even particularly close with—didn't invite me to her birthday party. It sounds small, maybe even silly. But I share it because some of the wounds we carry live in places too tender or too embarrassing to name. Offense doesn't always come in loud, obvious moments. Sometimes it comes quietly, through something as ordinary as exclusion.

That same week, this woman had come over for dinner with her kids. Everything seemed normal—warm, even. We laughed, shared stories, did life like women do. Then a few days later, I saw the photos: the party, the smiling faces, the circle I wasn't in. And something in me sank.

I couldn't stop wondering, Had I done something wrong? Should I say something? Would that make me seem insecure? Immature? I didn't ask. I just pulled away. I created distance, trying to protect myself from what felt like rejection, but the wound stayed. Because distance doesn't heal our hearts. Pretending not to care doesn't make the pain go away. Acting strong doesn't erase the sting. Only God can do that. Only God can get to the places we've hidden and bring healing where we've been silently hurting.

We need to admit our hurt, no matter how small. And eventually, as we practice living in the light and letting go, situations like this won't have the same power to move us as they once did. But for now, I will admit that they still do. Betrayal hurts. The slight did what slights do.

The truth is, I have probably made someone else feel the same way that woman made me feel. We have all done something like this to someone else: left them out unintentionally or intentionally, said something careless, ignored a need, or caused offense. None of us are the exception. We may not have hurt anyone to the extent we have been hurt by others, but we have all sinned, we all need God, and we all need wild forgiveness.

When we are hurt by someone, we have an immediate instinct to pull back and withdraw. Instead of leaning in to heal, we pick up offense. It takes self-awareness and what I call "identity work"—knowing who we are, having confidence in God's power in us—in order to have honest conversations and begin to heal in the ways God wants for us. There are layers to this that involve examining our assumptions and placing some boundaries, because at the end of the day, no one but God should have the power to determine our value or define our worth.

You might be feeling defensive at this point, arguing, "Well, yes, but my situation is complicated." It's true. Every situation is different. Every hurt has a right to be felt. You can be honest about the offense you feel. You deserve the space to grieve the things that have happened to you, but even more, you deserve to grow and heal from those hurts, with God by your side.

"You don't get it." I might not, but Jesus does.

"I'm scared to look at my pain." You'll repeat what you don't repair.

"I'm too far gone." Your life is too precious not to heal.

"They don't deserve forgiveness." You don't deserve to live with this unforgiveness.

"If I let go of my pain, I don't know what I have left." Your pain is not your identity.

"I can't come back from this." God won't leave you where He found you.

"I'll never forget what happened to me." Jesus is not asking you to forget. He wants to give you victory in your most wounded parts.

The Outrage of Offense

In chapter 1, we began to name our hurt and explore the nature of living from offense. It's more than a moment—it's a strategy. Crafty and quiet. Like a snake coiled beneath the brush, ready to strike. Like a fox slipping through the vineyard, looking for what it can steal. Like a vine twisting around an olive branch, slowly choking the life from it. Like weeds overtaking a once-beautiful garden. In the New Testament, the word "offense" comes from the Greek word *skandalon*—a word used to describe a snare, a trap, a stumbling block.[1] It was the part of a baited animal trap that triggered the catch. That's what offense does. It entices, entraps, and eventually entangles. And unless we learn to recognize it, we'll keep stumbling into the same pain, wondering why we still feel stuck.

Offense is a stumbling block in the way of abundant life, a trap set up conveniently and strategically, an obstacle making sure we're taken off course, off the path and purpose of our

---

1. Strong's Lexicon, "skandalon," BibleHub, accessed November 1, 2024, https://biblehub.com/greek/4625.htm.

lives. Offense is the snare that wraps us up, and it thrives off pride and grows in time.

Being offended is human. It's a moment—sharp, real, often justified. But living offended? That's a slow erosion of the soul. It's the quiet choice to carry what was meant to be released. The longer we hold on to offense, the more it shapes our vision, our voice, and the way we move through the world. That's where the real trap begins—not in what was done to us but in what we let linger within us, affecting our spiritual and emotional life. Offense is the hidden trap that tells us we're the exception—we're too hurt to heal, too right to release, too justified to let go. It whispers that we're the ones who have to carry out justice, that unless we hold on, we'll lose control. But in the process, we lose peace. Offense isolates us in our pain, blinds us to the future we could have, and quietly keeps us stuck.

To sum it up, being offended is a reaction. Living offended is a mindset and a trap—and it will shape your life if you let it.

Let's dig even deeper into the definition of offense. In a figurative sense, "offense" in Greek refers to anything that may cause a person to go astray from the path of righteousness or that may lead them into moral or spiritual error. Certain actions, attitudes, or teachings can create a snare for us, hindering our relationship with God or causing us to question our faith. The *Merriam-Webster Dictionary* defines offense as "something that outrages the moral or physical senses."[2]

The relationship between my dad and me was full of hurt, offense, and outrage. As I sit down to write these words at thirty-four years old, I realize I've spent more of my life in outrage than in peace, more in anger than in joy, more in envy

---

2. *Merriam-Webster Dictionary*, "offense," accessed November 1, 2024, https://www.merriam-webster.com/dictionary/offense.

than in confidence. Offense settled into my heart quietly, like a seed preparing to grow into weeds, until it shaped the way I saw everything. For years, I told my husband, counselors, and close friends that my early childhood had little effect on me. That I'd forgiven my dad for the wounds he'd left behind. That I understood him—he was a broken man with a wounded soul—and that his actions weren't a personal attack. And while that explanation gave me something to hold on to, it was only a fraction of what I needed to fully let go. Understanding his pain didn't heal mine.

Explaining our pain away doesn't work. Understanding helps, but it doesn't heal. It won't negate the emotional trauma or change what happened.

I want to offer you a moment to breathe here and remind you that this may be the holiest work you ever do. To slowly walk through this healing with God. To learn to deal with offense before it deals with you. To learn how to walk into a relationship or room and be ready to face whatever comes your way, and leave just as steady, clear, and secure as when you walked in. To peel back the layers with Him, to trust Him with your heart, even if just a little. I want to help you put down your defenses.

Picking up offense means choosing to hold on to resentment, dwelling on all the wrongs done to us, and letting them fester, which then shapes how we see ourselves and others. It impacts every part of us, including our relationships, thoughts, emotions, and actions. This weighs us down and stunts our personal and spiritual growth, ultimately blocking the path to healing. When we pick up offense, we are picking up a double-edged sword, with one side pointed out at others and one side pointed in toward ourselves. When we grip the handle of this sword:

- It keeps us from showing love and letting ourselves experience love in return.
- It makes us chase acceptance instead of living like we already have it.
- It stirs up insecurity and suspicion.
- It builds walls where we desperately need connection.

Offense might feel protective, but it's a trap. And maybe it's time we let it go.

Pain is an unavoidable part of the human experience; it's woven into the fabric of being alive. But while we can't escape it, we have the power to choose how we heal. We can confront our wounds without letting them dictate who we are—not forgetting the hurt or pretending it never existed, but rather refusing to let it have the final word, choosing instead to live in the freedom we were always meant to walk in.

Healing from the Hurt

Learning to surrender my hurt to God and allow Him to heal me is a journey unlike any other I've known. For so long, I've known only how to think about my pain, how to journal through it, and how to barely process it. But to truly let it go? That felt beyond me. How much journaling and processing until the pain went away? The anger and resentment I carried were so deep, so fierce, that they stole years of my life, robbing me of confidence in my calling and security in who God created me to be. They stripped me of love, turning vulnerability into an enemy. I let the rejection of others ensnare me, and the less I lived in the truth of God's love, the less love I could see and receive. The more I let the wounds of my past define my story, the more defeated I became. Instead of running toward God, I ran from Him. Hurt has a way of making us feel so alone, so desperate, that we find ourselves fleeing from healing and the freedom God offers.

In Luke 15:11–32, we read the parable about the prodigal son. A father had two sons, and the younger son approached his father and asked for his share of the inheritance, essentially wishing his father was already dead. The father, heartbroken but respecting his son's decision, divided his property between his two sons. The younger one then squandered his wealth in wild living and eventually found himself impoverished and desperate. Realizing his mistakes, he decided to return to his father, hoping to be accepted as a servant, since he now considered himself unworthy of being called his father's son.

However, as the son approached, the father saw him from a distance and ran to him, embracing him with love and joy. The father even celebrated his return by throwing him a grand feast.

This is how God loves us. Can you see it? Do you feel it? A son overwhelmed by the weight of his sin, yet being embraced by a father interested only in restoration. Meanwhile, the older son stood outside the celebration—offended, overlooked, and quietly resentful. He had done everything right, yet it didn't feel like enough. This is how pride and bitterness often take root—not in rebellion, but in the belief that our goodness has gone unnoticed. The older son wasn't angry because his brother had come home; he was angry because grace was given freely, and he had been working to earn it all along. He was envious. Insecure. Afraid of not being loved.

Pride makes it easy to call offense a home. When the father heard about his older son's offense, he went to him and explained that *everything* he had belonged to his son as well. The older son was missing nothing! All the love, safety, and security he was looking for were already his.

They're ours too. They're all already ours. The love, the acceptance, the security and safety. We don't have to fight for them or take offense to prove that they are ours or that we are His.

The father reassured his older son of his love and reminded him of the importance of forgiveness and rejoicing over his brother's return. He knew that in order for the offense to be mended, love would have to lead the way, along with softness, humility, and compassion. You can't beat offense with offense, hurt with hurt, or unforgiveness with unforgiveness—only love. Only living out of that love, and not for it.

The parable ends with the father's plea for the older son to let go of his offense and celebrate the restoration of their family, presenting a beautiful and brave picture of forgiveness. It highlights the father's love and grace toward both his wayward son and his faithful son. The parable is messy and beautiful and even exposes some of our own pride. The father isn't worried about fairness or who is right but about the wholeness and restoration of both sons' hearts.

God's love does the same for us—it mends what only He can mend. He reconciles situations and offenses that feel too far gone, even the ones we can't make sense of. The Father's love changes everything. It looks at our wounds and speaks directly to them. He does not leave us in our hurt.

Sit with that for just a second. It was time with the father that helped heal the younger son's wounds, not time on his own.

Harboring offense can prevent us from experiencing the joy of reconciliation and the transformative power of forgiveness and grace. While offense and trauma are distinct, it is important to note that repeated or severe offenses, especially if they involve abusive or harmful actions, can contribute to the development of trauma. This is why you and I, my friend, must learn how to let go of hurt and offense.

Learning to let go and dealing with offense are different from anything else I have ever had to walk through. Time alone won't heal my wounds, but time with God will.

I can't tough it out, fight it out, or ignore the hurt. I've tried. I can't make others pay for what they've done; trying to has only made me pay for it through years of bitterness, resentment, envy, and defeat. It has only forced me to live stuck in offense and unforgiveness, praying for a different outcome but held hostage by stubborn wounds.

We can't heal at will, but we can heal with God. This process isn't about becoming someone who doesn't care about our hurt or pain; it's about becoming people who care so deeply about our souls and experiencing everything God has for us that we know what deserves the most time and effort. Learning to not pick up offense requires believing that God took the weight of the world on His own shoulders, through Jesus, so we wouldn't have to.

When we are unaware of where we stand with our pain and offense, even the smallest slight can feel like a personal attack. Over time, we stack up our hurts and build coping mechanisms to survive them, but they never truly work. We ruminate and run ourselves ragged trying to make sense of the offense and pain, desperately searching for reasons that may never come. But the truth is, we will never fully comprehend evil, nor will we ever make sense of what is incomprehensible. Healing isn't found in understanding; it's found in surrender.

Rather than ruminating on or distracting ourselves from the pain and offense, we must learn to move through them with God. Healing begins when we accept what we cannot change, surrender the hurt, and invite God into the mess. People may hurt us, but their actions don't have to define us. With God, we can release the pain, move forward, and step into the freedom we've been searching for. Offense and pain don't need to be our master—we can choose to release them and let God instead of the hurt define us. This is the key to the freedom we've all been looking for.

I've tried to think about the last two decades of my life with intention, searching for all the little hurts that I have picked up—the little hurts that have made me less loving and more protective, defensive, and suspicious. The ones that stole my confidence. The ones that dimmed my light.

I am the woman I am because of the circumstances I have walked through. You are who you are because of the paths and winding roads you have taken in life. We wear our pain, our insecurities, and our resentment. We wear our unhealed wounds and defensiveness. We wear them like a cloak of protection from those around us. Ill-equipped, we wound those around us with our brittle and battered hearts. When we recognize the bruises we have gained along the way, we can finally begin to address how they have shaped us.

Loving Others Too

I am not the only one living with hurt. Those around us have their own bruises too. With all the self-help advice our culture throws at us, there is still a crucial piece missing from the equation: love for others, empathy, a true understanding of our humanity, and a foundation rooted in how we're called to live in God's kingdom.

I fear we've become so hyperfocused on self-healing that we've lost sight of the command to love our neighbor—not just as we love ourselves (Mark 12:31) but as God has loved us (John 13:34). Perhaps how we respond to others says more about our relationship with God than it does about them. Can we offer a love we have not received ourselves?

This book is about you, but it is also about your neighbor. I want to take the load off and offer a way forward so your soul can breathe honestly and exhale safely. The work of feeling safe enough with God to feel and heal is what we're engaging in, and this journey not only frees you but also enables you to love others from that place of healing.

Here are a few verses to help you feel safe and secure with God before we move forward. Take a moment to read through each verse, asking God to settle and seal this truth in you.

> God is our refuge and strength,
> a helper who is always found
> in times of trouble. (Ps. 46:1)

> Do not fear, for I am with you;
> do not be afraid, for I am your God.
> I will strengthen you; I will help you;
> I will hold on to you with my righteous right hand.
>   (Isa. 41:10)

> The LORD is my rock and my fortress and my savior,
> My God, my rock, in whom I take refuge;

> My shield and the horn of my salvation, my
> stronghold.
> I call upon the LORD, who is worthy to be praised,
> And I am saved from my enemies. (Ps. 18:2–3 NASB)

For I am persuaded that neither death nor life, nor angels nor rulers, nor things present nor things to come, nor powers, nor height nor depth, nor any other created thing will be able to separate us from the love of God that is in Christ Jesus our Lord. (Rom. 8:38–39)

> The LORD will protect you from all harm;
> he will protect your life.
> The LORD will protect your coming and going
> both now and forever. (Ps. 121:7–8)

The Roads We've Walked

The roads we've walked shape the way we respond to offense. Along the path, we've picked up ways to manage, cope with, and tend to our hurt. All these traps begin in our minds, fueled by the imagination and creativity we possess, and they work hard to ensure their own survival. Unnoticed at first, offense gathers little gods—false sources of confidence and courage. It weaves stories and creates narratives we start to believe, even when they are false. It's prideful to pretend the offense hasn't hurt us, and even more so to think we can do this holy work of letting go without God.

In this journey of learning to let go, we must explore the beliefs that have kept us bound. To truly step into the life God has for us, we need to let go of the things that have kept us stuck in this hidden trap of offense. If we don't, we'll continue to carry the weight of it. But here's the good news: There's a way forward. We don't have to remain in the dark. We can choose to turn on the light, allowing God to illuminate the truth, heal our wounds, and set us free from what has kept us captive. Only then can we truly begin to live in the fullness of what He has called us to.

Turn On the Light

Whenever anyone has offended me, I try to raise my soul so high that the offense cannot reach it.

René Descartes

Offense has a way of turning the light off in our souls, our faith life, and our thought life. We go dark from the pain and wounding we have been nursing for so long. We go dark from the unmet expectations and betrayal, from the disappointment and despair. In the dark, our wounds grow and our offense festers into what they have become today or will become tomorrow.

Have you ever walked into a dark room and tried to feel your way through instead of turning on the light? Unless you're familiar with the landscape, you'll spend most of your time running into things, trying to find your way out, or searching feverishly for the light switch. Arms outstretched, you feel for safety and stability. You use all your senses to try to make your way to the light. It's unnerving, but you do your best to stay calm. It's just a dark room, right?

The fear isn't the room itself or the darkness. It's the lack of control we experience when the tools we have to navigate through it feel insufficient. We fear a lack of control. We fear the threat of pain.

This is how I see offense play out. It's not superficial—it's a defense mechanism we develop to handle the pain we've carried. It's our way of saying, "This hurt." Our flesh reacts to protect our beliefs and the boundaries we feel have been crossed. It knows what to do here. Once we've been wounded, the mind does whatever it takes to shield us from more pain. The less secure we feel, the more we perceive being taken advantage of, and the more offense we store up. We are walking into dark rooms every day when we carry our offense.

In the beginning, God created the heavens and earth. He noticed that darkness covered the surface of the water and saw the need for there to be light. It was the second thing God did after creating heaven and earth: He gave us light to see and grow in (Gen. 1:1–4). Since the beginning, He knew we couldn't function in the dark, physically or metaphorically. Darkness isn't where we grow; it's where things normally go to die. It's the beginning of the end, if we choose to remain in it. And although God can and will use these dark seasons to heal us, we were made to grow in the *light*. Without the sun, we would lose life on earth. In the light is the place where the wounds heal.

It's time to pray for the courage to turn on the light.

Turning On the Light

I couldn't get out of bed. It wasn't just a bad day or a hard morning—it was a terrible season. "I'm so tired of having hard seasons," I whispered to myself as tears streamed down my cheeks. There weren't enough words to piece together the pain that had become this complicated web of reality. Everything felt hard. Sometimes life feels so heavy, and all you can do is sigh.

In these moments, I struggled with feeling weak for simply being human, like the woman who can't seem to pull herself together. I put on my Amazon slippers—a recent buy to bring in a little happy, because we all need a little happy—and walked over to the mirror to catch a glimpse of the woman staring back. I splashed cold water on my face, hoping it would calm me down. I'd read somewhere that it helps regulate the vagus nerve. And my nerves needed regulating—all of them.

But even the under-eye patches I bought wouldn't hide the puffiness from my tears. I was tired. My soul was tired. I'd been using every tool I'd learned to try to move through this offense, but none of them seemed to be working. Mario and I were having a hard time communicating. We were in the middle of COVID, the church we were part of was imploding, and my dad was trying to reconnect.

How could I heal from childhood wounds while raising children? How could I lead in a church filled with people who felt like they'd become enemies overnight? How were God and I doing? What in the world did authentic discipleship even look like? And could someone please tell me how to be friends as an adult? Was I okay?

I was more upset with myself than anyone else for being back in the darkness again. I felt helpless and stuck, and willing myself out of it wasn't enough. It could have been depression again. Maybe I was just exasperated at how unsafe I felt, how rejected I'd been living, or how exhausting it was to be the only one fighting for myself.

I got up and tried to go about my day. I took the next step and glanced at my phone calendar. I had a counseling appointment coming up—perfect timing.

During my counseling session, I sat down and started with a brief recap of the week, letting the story of my dad slip out: the memory of him asking me to make him a drink. So much of the offense I didn't know needed healing started to show itself. I tried to make sense of it again, and of him maybe being a part of my life somehow.

It wasn't my first time seeing this particular counselor. I continued talking about how my dad, a high-functioning alcoholic I barely knew, left a trail of pain behind him. I wanted to fully understand how to love him, but it was complicated. The sharp edges of his brokenness cut deep, hurting those around him and leaving me with my own scars. Hurt people hurt people, and his pain had become my pain. I didn't remember feeling safe enough to be a child; instead, I remembered always needing to be brave. It was a weight I had carried, trying to save everyone and everything around me, ever since.

My counselor listened and nodded. "How did that make you feel?" she asked.

I was good at explaining the hurt away. I wanted to be perceived as someone wise and strong, unoffendable. It felt like a badge of honor. But I responded with honesty. "Rejected. Unloved. Hurt."

The very emotions that made me want to hide under my covers spun me into a spiral of shame. If I admitted that I'd been carrying offenses around, then maybe I would have to face whatever else was underneath the hood of my heart.

But maybe peeling back the layers was the next step. Maybe God was here, wanting me to experience more grace, more love on the other side of this pain. Maybe the end of myself was the best place to begin again.

Then my counselor asked, "How do you think that impacts you today?"

For the love of God. Not today. I sighed. I was tired of looking, of finding, of growing at the expense of the pain others had caused me. I even felt bitter about getting better.

These were my options:

1. I could tell her I was fine and I was here only to tell people I'm healing, to tell them the right thing.
2. I could engage deeply with my wounds and finally learn to let go.

I ground my teeth. My pride and fear rose up. But it was time.

"I want to be loved and accepted. I have the propensity to work for both. I want my leadership's affirmation. I want people to think and *know* that I'm enough. I've never felt fully loved and only know love as a currency that's based on my efficiency. I have lived with hurt feelings my whole life, and today is no different. I feel like I will forever have to protect myself."

I was angry. With each word came more indignation. Embarrassment flooded my heart. I hated sharing my story: a broken home, a young girl looking for love in all the wrong places and plagued by debilitating depression, chaos and offense braided into this life of mine that I wished away. As much as I wanted a different story or life, this was mine to own, to grow in, to heal in. Mine in which to see the purpose God had so divinely set apart for me. There is beauty in even the broken pieces. And truth be told, it isn't the silver lining that heals us but the journey there with God. His presence in the middle with us is what mends us.

The floodgates were opened. This led to uncharted wounds and emotions, the ones I'd worked so hard to downplay. They were the background singers in the song of my life, and it was time to listen closely.

I avoided eye contact with my counselor and said, "I don't want to believe this, but I do feel like I am the sum total of the past and pain, and no matter how much I try to outrun them, it feels impossible to leave them behind. I don't believe it's totally true, but my whole life feels like I'm a project for God."

I knew that my dad's reality no longer had to be mine, but I had picked up his offense like a souvenir. If knowing the genesis of our stories and our wounds helps us break free from the vines that grip us, then it was time to face my own. Earlier that week, I had landed on a phone call with my dad. He wanted to visit and see his grandchildren. I was paralyzed. Should I let him back into our lives? Was he actually ever in them?

"I'd love to drive down and see you and the kids," he'd said. This was a huge step for him, and it would be an act of courage for us. In the past, I had held firm boundaries between my dad and my family. I went no contact for a while, then we tiptoed back into a relationship. I would occasionally call and say hi. The kids barely knew him, and that was on purpose.

He seemed to be in a healthier headspace now. He was older and maybe more aware of the time he had left. I talked to Mario about the potential visit, and we agreed that maybe we'd give it a try, just once.

"Of course you can come down. We'd love to see you," I told my dad.

It doesn't always work out this way. But for me, seeing my dad was an essential step as I learned to let go of false and hurtful narratives that played on a loop in my heart. I didn't want my hurt to define me or my future. I didn't want to live with this anger anymore. God wanted to and could heal this hurt. The question was, would I let Him? I knew that was my first step in choosing to forgive and to practice forgiving my dad again.

God sees our wounds and knows how to restore them. He sees our hearts and knows how to piece them back together. And when we turn on the light, we notice that we've been carrying words, situations, and circumstances around as our compass.

When the light of our soul is turned off, when our thought life is left to wander in the dark, when our faith life is operating in despair and defeat, we are left exposed to the sin that grows when no one is looking.

An Attacked Faith Life

Do you know what attacks our faith life more than anything? The love of self. In Genesis 3, Satan introduced Adam and Eve to the same pride he struggled with. Satan was deeply offended by God, jealous of His beauty and authority. His desire to be better than God overflowed in offense to everyone around him. He lived offended with God and brought others along with him. The enemy offered Adam and Eve a way to be like God, imitating his glory and power. He made an idol out of becoming like God and offered it to everyone who would listen.

> I will ascend into heaven,
> I will exalt my throne above the stars of God;
> I will also sit on the mount of the congregation
> On the farthest sides of the north;
> I will ascend above the heights of the clouds,
> I will be like the Most High. (Isa. 14:13–14 NKJV)

I've felt the pull of wanting to choose God but loving what the world has to offer just a little too much. Surrender—flipping on the light—was the only way out for me.

Offense, though, is like fertile soil for little gods to grow. When we're hurt by others, or even when we feel let down by God Himself, we start looking for something to fill the void.

Offense leaves us feeling vulnerable, unloved, overlooked, undervalued, misplaced, and misunderstood. The hurt just hurts. And trying to make peace with the pain? It can leave us searching for love in all the wrong places. We get rejected by a group of friends, and suddenly we're chasing the approval of others. We're overlooked for a promotion, and now it's all we can think about. We pour ourselves into proving our worth, turning that "no" or "not yet" into an idol we can't put down. Sometimes self-righteousness sneaks in too. It feels like a badge of honor, something we can cling to, promising we'll do whatever it takes to make sure we avoid this pain ever happening again. But the truth? It only ties us tighter to our offense. The pain becomes the compass of our soul, steering us toward building little kingdoms with little gods where we're the ones in charge.

I want us to heal. To really heal. To see the light again—to feel the joy and contentment of life, to find our way back to God. To understand how these hurts have shaped us into people we don't even recognize—and definitely don't want to be. Because the offense doesn't just wound us; it keeps us from becoming the women we were made to be. The women we *long* to be.

Letting Go of Pride

Pride deceives us into believing that healing depends on an apology and resolution, on the other person's repentance. Yet true healing happens only when we surrender our hurt to Jesus. When we're grounded in Him, we stop living at the mercy of our pain. We step out of the shadows of offense, finding the freedom to live fully loved and unshaken. We can do it. With God, we can step into healing and let go.

I hate to say it or confess it, but offended people tend to be the most prideful people. Coming from a woman who knows this to be true, I can tell you that I've missed God's abundance most in my life when I've been preoccupied with the sin and offense of others toward me, and not my own wretched wrongs. I've been most wrong in friendships and in my marriage when I couldn't look past my pain to see the hearts of those around me.

When offense blinds us, it locks our focus onto the wounds others have caused. It blinded me in ways I'm still untangling, creating agreements with insecurity, bitterness, and resentment that held me hostage. Offense took the light out of my eyes, dimming the world around me, and left me wondering if I'd ever feel alive again. When I let go of my pride and admit my flaws, I not only make room for forgiveness, but I open myself up to a deeper, richer love.

Real healing begins when we allow God to hold up a mirror and show us the places within us that need grace. And here is where we receive true abundance—not in the absence of the hurt but in the presence of God in it. When we let God heal the hurt in our hearts, the first thing to go is our pride. We realize just how deeply we've needed Him—and in that, we discover how loved, forgiven, and valued we are in His eyes.

In the Middle of Offense

I sat in the middle of offense for a long time, too long, allowing it to steal so much of my life. It truly was my biggest roadblock, and I couldn't see it. I could see the pain caused by others, that was clear. But the choice to stay in it I was blind to.

Offense lures us into believing that others hold the key to our peace, but in reality, our pride is what keeps these idols—our need for approval, validation, control—alive in our hearts. In moments of hurt, we're invited to seek God, but in offense, we're tempted to look inward. Hurt reveals the depth of our wounds, while offense reveals how unhealed we still are. It serves as a powerful gauge for how secure we are in Christ and who we are in Him. And when we truly begin to heal with Jesus, we stop living at the mercy of others and every hurt that comes our way.

What might it look like if, instead of being offended by the actions of others, you embraced the truth that their treatment of you doesn't define you? What if you could heal your hurt with God without letting it manage you? Imagine if, when someone rejected you, it didn't send you spiraling into shame. What if their betrayal, instead of consuming you, became the very space where God could meet you in healing and strength?

Sometimes the sting of offense reveals deeper, untended wounds. And God, in His grace, shows us where we need healing and brings vindication. He reconciles what we cannot, giving us the eyes not only to see beyond our hurt but also to truly see our hurt. He enables us to face the pain in our lives without letting it define us. He invites us to feel it fully and recognize how much love exists for even the broken parts of us. That's the real miracle: God walking beside us in our pain.

The Attack of Offense

Offense keeps us trapped, dancing in our pain and replaying our hurts rather than healing from them. The enemy knows that when we're consumed by offense, we're less open to God's voice and more drawn to our own pride, feeling justified in our pain. It's not a harmless crime when we carry offense. It attacks:

> *Our relationships with others.* When we harbor offense, it becomes difficult to maintain healthy, loving relationships with others. This can isolate us from the community in every way. "A brother wronged is more unyielding than a fortified city; disputes are like the barred gates of a citadel" (Prov. 18:19 NIV).
>
> *Our relationship with God.* Holding on to offense can create a barrier between us and God. It can hinder our prayers and worship, as our hearts are not fully aligned

with God's will of forgiveness and love. "When you stand praying, if you hold anything against anyone, forgive them, so that your Father in heaven may forgive you your sins" (Mark 11:25 NIV).

Our own hearts. If not dealt with, offense can turn into bitterness and resentment. These negative emotions can consume our thoughts and affect our attitude toward others and God, leading to a hardened heart. "See to it that no one falls short of the grace of God and that no bitter root grows up to cause trouble and defile many" (Heb. 12:15 NIV).

Our purpose. Focusing on offenses can distract us from God's purpose and calling in our lives. It can lead us to dwell on the past and on negative experiences rather than moving forward in faith and obedience. "Brothers and sisters, I do not consider myself yet to have taken hold of it. But one thing I do: Forgetting what is behind and straining toward what is ahead, I press on toward the goal to win the prize for which God has called me heavenward in Christ Jesus" (Phil. 3:13–14 NIV).

Our spiritual growth. Spiritual growth requires a heart that is open and receptive to the Holy Spirit. Offense can stifle this growth by filling our hearts with resentment and bitterness and blocking the work of the Holy Spirit. "Do not grieve the Holy Spirit of God, with whom you were sealed for the day of redemption. Get rid of all bitterness, rage and anger, brawling and slander, along with every form of malice. Be kind and compassionate to one another, forgiving each other, just as in Christ God forgave you" (Eph. 4:30–32 NIV).

Our behavior. Offense can provoke sinful reactions such as anger, retaliation, and gossip. These behaviors are contrary to the teachings of Christ and can lead us further away from living a righteous life. "My dear brothers and sisters, take note of this: Everyone should be quick to listen, slow to speak and slow to become angry, because human anger does not produce the righteousness that God desires" (James 1:19–20 NIV).

Our trust in God. Constantly feeling offended can weaken our faith and trust in God. We might begin to question God's justice and goodness, leading to doubt and a weakened faith. "When my heart was grieved and my spirit embittered, I was senseless and ignorant; I was a brute beast before you" (Ps. 73:21–22 NIV).

The offense can be obvious or subtle, but one thing is consistent: The enemy wants to use it to attack every part of our lives. We must pay attention to the bait he uses to lure us into the trap: our thoughts, where it all begins. This is why we must let go and *can* let go, turning the page to the new day ahead. We can be brave enough to start again, with God.

A Compromised Thought Life

Learning to let go begins with an honest, sometimes uncomfortable look at the lies, thoughts, and limiting beliefs we've unknowingly gathered along the way. These beliefs, often hidden beneath the layers of our hurt, become like heavy baggage we carry with us, shaping how we respond to offense and weighing down our hearts. The path to healing starts with facing these beliefs head-on and realigning our thoughts with the truth of who God says we are.

Making peace with our pain requires us to courageously shine a light on it to see where it's truly hiding. It's fascinating to realize that emotional pain—whether from rejection or broken relationships—activates the same areas of the brain as physical pain, such as the anterior insula and anterior cingulate cortex. In fact, research shows that something as simple as acetaminophen can dull emotional pain, reducing activity in these very brain regions.

But here's the question we all need to ask ourselves: What are we using to numb the pain of our offense?

When we find something that offers temporary relief—whether it's avoiding the pain, denying the pain, getting angry, or even overspiritualizing our hurt—we tend to cling to it, hoping it will heal us. Yet we know in our hearts that these quick fixes rarely bring lasting healing. Instead, they can deepen our wounds, distort our thoughts, and create a breeding ground for destructive habits, self-justification, and false beliefs.

This is where the fight begins. Offense feeds on the thoughts we allow to linger. Unchecked lies—like "I'm not enough," "I'll always be hurt," or "They owe me"—can become the soundtrack of our minds, shaping our perspective of ourselves, others, and even God.

Scripture beautifully calls us to renew our minds (Rom. 12:2) and take every thought captive (2 Cor. 10:5), because our thought life is where offense either takes root or gets uprooted. Healing begins when we bravely uncover the lies we've believed and exchange them for the truth of God's Word.

For me, it started with questions: *What am I carrying in my heart? Are these thoughts true? Are they from Christ?* For so long, I held on to lies as if they were my own. My inner world felt like a constant ache, replaying memories of my dad's anger, memories of my mom's sadness, and a longing to feel the love I thought others received more freely than I did. Those feelings shaped how I saw everything. But as I allowed God's truth to settle in, it was like a soothing balm for my soul, gently replacing the chaos with His steady, loving voice. As I began to process all of this with God, I found myself asking some honest questions—ones that might help you too:

- What thoughts am I nursing that are keeping me stuck in offense?
- Am I filtering my pain through God's truth or my hurt?
- How can I align my thoughts with His promises today?

The fight for our thought life is the fight for our freedom.

Limiting Beliefs

Limiting beliefs are thoughts we've accepted as truth that distort what we believe about God, His Word, and ourselves. These beliefs shape how we see the world as a whole, and even how and when we take up offense. Take Adam and Eve, for example. Satan didn't just question God's command; he twisted Adam and Eve's understanding of God's character. His lie planted doubts about God's goodness and trustworthiness, which invited their disobedience. When we allow limiting beliefs to take root, we do the same. We limit God to the confines of our experiences, centering Him in *our* story instead of recognizing that we are part of *His*.

In other words, when we confine God to the pain and hurt we've endured, we rob ourselves of knowing Him beyond those circumstances. But God is so much greater than our wounds, our fears, and our disappointments. His truth invites us to step outside the boundaries of our limiting beliefs and experience the fullness of who He is.

Letting go of offense requires us to confront these beliefs and ask, *What am I believing about God that isn't true? How is this shaping how I see myself and others?* The more we align our thoughts with His Word, the less power offense has over us and the more freedom we find in His love.

God sees our wounds and knows how to restore them. He sees our hearts and knows how to piece them back together.

Peter, a disciple of Jesus and a pillar of the Christian faith, saw Jesus perform miracles and witnessed the transformation of lives. But he also experienced storms—both physical and spiritual—and in his humanness, he denied Jesus in front of others (Matt. 26:70–74).

Oh, Peter, how I can relate! I have seen Him move, our Jesus, but sometimes the storms are just so blinding.

We shouldn't jump to conclusions and judge the intent of Peter's heart. However, from the context, we can guess that one reason Peter denied Jesus was out of fear. We can perhaps even say it was fear of death, fear of rejection, fear of being an outcast, or fear of being let down. Perhaps he wondered if the liberation that Jesus promised was falling apart. I think Peter was deeply afraid that Jesus didn't have his best interests at heart, that maybe Jesus wasn't who He said He was, and that death would have the last say. The enemy will present us with similar thoughts, and how we respond to this snare, this offense, is the key to learning to let go.

What can we learn from Peter at this moment? Why did he respond this way? I think Peter was tangled up in the weeds of limiting beliefs about God and wrapped up in lies surrounding His power.

Overcoming Limiting Beliefs

I began to overcome limiting beliefs as I embraced more of God's truth and surrendered my deep-rooted assumptions. My experiences were no longer the compass or thermostat for how I allowed myself to react or navigate life. Instead, God's truth became my loving guide.

What we believe about God informs who we are and how we see the world. When we let go of the stories shaped by our own fears and past hurts, we make room for God's perspective to transform us. This shift empowers us to live with clarity, confidence, and peace, rooted in His unchanging love.

Pause for a moment and think of God as:

Father (2 Cor. 6:18)
Creator (Ps. 139)
Savior (Eph. 2:5)
Friend (John 15:15)
Counselor (John 14:16–17, 26)

This is who God is—our foundation and compass, our refuge and friend when we are hurting. We are safe with God, and He can help us move through even the deepest offense.

Being guided by *His* Word and *His* truth can provide us with an immovable sense of security if we let it. We can be anchored in eternal truth, breaking off the roots of the beliefs that used to limit us. Often our emotions keep us from seeing offense through a gospel-shaped lens.

Jesus told Peter that he would deny Him, and yet Jesus still loved him. The lessons are endless here. In short, what Peter believed about Jesus informed how he responded, but he let the fear of being persecuted and rejected be his guide.

When we live in fear of being offended, we end up shackled to its control. When fear of offense controls us, it becomes us. Offense has a way of leaving its mark on us like black ink that spreads, touching everything in its path. To understand just how deeply offense runs in our own hearts, we have to ask ourselves, *What do I believe about myself and why? What do I believe about God? What do I believe about His posture toward me? Where are these beliefs coming from?*

Experiencing the fullness of God's grace in my life required letting go of offense. I discovered that it was easier to love my dad wholeheartedly when I wasn't burdened by disappointment and resentment. Instead of letting those feelings guide me, I allowed God's love for both of us to be my compass.

Healing the Hidden Places

My youngest daughter convinced me to buy a snow globe from the Target dollar aisle a few years ago. It was just the right size for her tiny hand. She loved how the snow fell inside it, and she carried it around so often that it always looked as though it was snowing. From her perspective, it was magical. "Mommy, look! It just keeps snowing!" she would say, eyes wide with wonder. I glanced at her hand cupping the tiny globe and smiled. Then I felt God gently whisper, "That's a lot like how your soul feels right now. I'm shaking it up, but it's a soft settling—I've got you. Pay attention to what's coming up. I'm doing a new thing."

I had been praying for healing, for peace. The offense I carried had wrapped itself around me like a suffocating vine. The more I prayed for God to heal me, the more the snowflakes kept falling in a never-ending storm. But that perpetual shaking was God's way of exposing the tangled roots and weeds where my soul had found false shelter. Pride, unforgiveness, anger, resentment, and my own sin had flourished in the perfect environment I had unknowingly provided.

Sometimes we all need a good shaking up, even—maybe especially—when we don't want it.

I worked in vocational ministry for over eight years, and even during the hardest moments, I cherished it: the people, the church. One way or another, we are called to serve the church and build her up (Eph. 4:16). In those eight years, I learned some of the most challenging lessons, all while anchored to the same God and within the same body of believers. I learned what it means to live from His love instead of for the approval of others. It was in that setting that the Refiner used fire to transform me and teach me how to love, even when others didn't acknowledge, appreciate, or even see me.

But even as I served, there were moments that the ache of unseen obedience surfaced. The bitterness didn't always show up loudly—sometimes it whispered beneath the surface. I remember the moment the words slipped out, raw and unfiltered: "That was supposed to be me."

I had moved from position to position, trying to follow God's assignments—most of the time. But somewhere in the movement, I started measuring my worth by the roles I had and the recognition I received.

God allows seasons of challenge and change to cultivate humility, sharpen faith, and teach us unbridled surrender. It's in these times that we learn to let go of our expectations and trust that His way is best—even when ours seemed right. In these moments, I began to see how my response to God was rooted in pride. How we respond to moments of offense reveals much about the condition of our relationship with Him. I had to learn how to not take everything personally but also remember that with God, it all is personal. He does not take lightly which way we should go, and each turn is a gift.

God wastes nothing. That means we aren't bound by the yes or no of others. We are not bound by cold shoulders or betrayal. Let that truth settle in.

Of course I wanted the job. I had worked tirelessly to be considered for the promotion. But I didn't get it. The embarrassment overwhelmed me. I had waited so long for this, and the disappointment was sharp. Trying to make sense of it all, I requested a meeting with my leaders. I needed to understand why I was being placed in a different position—one I hadn't asked for—instead of the one I had naturally expected to step into. Their words still echo in my memory: "We just don't need you there; we need you here." That sentence landed like a weight. I nodded politely, but inside, I felt unseen, passed over, and quietly heartbroken.

When we place idols—whether they are achievements, people, or security—on the throne of our hearts, we lose sight of God and who we are in Him. I knew that breaking free from the grip of offense meant examining why it had such a hold on me in the first place.

It felt as though I was being pushed out. All my insecurities surfaced, including ones I thought I had already healed from.

This last role change felt like a demotion. They said it wasn't, but it felt that way.

Every hurt is an opportunity for God to reveal more about ourselves and to invite us into obedience and surrender. Some of the worst things we can do are assume we know why people make the choices they do, assume we know why they may not like or support us, and create narratives in our heads based on our own limited perspective.

I found myself in a role that wasn't aligned with my passions or natural strengths. *Don't they see all that I have to offer? Why am I here?* These questions became fertile ground for the enemy and a breeding ground for offense. But one lesson stood out from this season: the opportunity to grow with God in both barren and bountiful times. It's in the barren seasons that God often cultivates His best work before any fruit appears. I took a moment to write down all the ways God was working in me, because I needed that tangible reminder. He was lovingly healing and growing me and refining my leadership in ways I hadn't experienced before. It wasn't a punishment; it was preparation.

Our identity isn't defined by what we do but by whose we are. We don't need to pick up offense when God has already carried the weight of that darkness and overcome the world (John 16:33).

Lessons on Offense from Jonah

I relate to the prophet Jonah when it comes to offense and pride. Remember the man who was swallowed up and spit out by a whale? God gave him clear instructions to go to Nineveh and preach against the people's wicked ways, with the goal of bringing about their repentance. God was offering grace and compassion toward the Ninevites, but Jonah detested them and did not want them to experience God's mercy. God then exposed Jonah's pride, his anger, and perhaps even his jealousy and bitterness (Jon. 4:1–3). When we place anything above God's love for us on the throne of our hearts, we become idolaters.

Jonah's disobedience led him to a ship where he was ultimately pushed overboard by the crew, who feared he was bad luck. To be clear, Jonah asked to be pushed overboard (Jon. 1:9–15). After he was thrown into the sea, God sent a whale to save his life. Not just his physical life but his spiritual life too. What followed were a few days of reflection and, ultimately, repentance. God gave Jonah three days and three nights in that whale. It wasn't until the third day that Jonah laid down his pride and sought God again.

There is always a third day when hope becomes our reality. Nothing is ever wasted with God.

"Then Jonah prayed to the LORD his God from the fish's belly. And he said: 'I cried out to the LORD because of my affliction, and He answered me. Out of the belly of Sheol I cried, and You heard my voice'" (Jon. 2:1–2 NKJV). The Hebrew *Sheol* can also be translated as "the grave." Jonah knew his life would be in the grave without God's intervention and redirection.

God is constantly intervening on our behalf. He often uses our physical circumstances to transform us spiritually. He wants to resurrect our souls and redeem them. Because Jesus rose, our souls can now rise with Him too.

Pride blinded Jonah from seeing God's heart and desire for him. God's no for him was because He had a better yes—one for Jonah's good, God's glory, and salvation for the lost.

But pride didn't allow Jonah to see what God was forming in Him.

When we live for Jesus, we are living for His dream to overflow through us, which means that our plans won't always go as we'd like—and that's good news. It means we won't always be treated fairly or rightly, yet we're called to sacrificial love. In His love, God often derails our plans before we destroy ourselves.

In John 5:1–9, there was a man who spent all his time by the pool of Bethesda, hoping to be healed. He had been lame for thirty-eight years, and he lived for the hope that someone might one day help him into the pool to receive his healing. His expectations were met with daily disappointment. First, he placed his expectations on what humans could do for him. Second, he put his faith in a superstition of his day. Thirty-eight years of unmet expectations most definitely caused him a lot of disappointment and discouragement—that is, until Jesus showed up. Until Jesus healed Him without using the pool and forgave his sins. Jesus redirected all his expectations forever.

When we exchange our unmet expectations, hurt feelings, or resentment for joy and humility, we begin to break free from offense and truly start the process of undoing the hold it has on us. Humility and trust are cultivated in the very seasons where pride once held sway. In this sacred exchange, we witness transformation as pride gives way to a deeper reliance on God and an openness to His shaping work in our lives.

When we're in the middle of offense, pride deceives us into thinking that our healing is in the hands of those who have hurt, rejected, and betrayed us. But when we heal with Jesus, we can finally release the hold our hurt has over us and move away from the offense and toward Christ.

I don't want you to look past the hurt but rather into it. Look at what the offense has done. Has it served you? Has it helped you?

Turn on the light, friend, because your wounds can't heal in the dark.

Break Free from Offense

Let the Grace In

Our greatest setback to letting go of offense won't be learning to forgive or even trying to forget, but letting God's grace heal us from the inside out.

One of the worst things about the pain we experience when we are rejected, betrayed, or slighted is the way it causes us to lose parts of ourselves. I don't actually know when it happened or how I started losing myself—my joy, my courage, my passion, my worth. It could be that the million little paper cuts of offense I'd been carrying finally became my identity. I don't want this to resonate with you, but if it does, don't worry. This is where it changes for us. We no longer want to wear the pain of offense. We are finished with repeating wrongs done and carrying around the weight of rejection. We are ready to let God's grace in—to let His love heal and mend us. We are walking out of the trap. We are cutting the weeds.

Let It Be What It Is, with God

Being raised by a single mom meant moving all the time. Instability was the constant thread of my youth. We never had enough, but somehow we made it through the darkest days of our lives. I saw the strongest woman I knew work from daybreak to sunset, juggling it all: multiple jobs, trips to the food banks, managing her own pain, and the stress of bills piling up.

Truthfully, I'm overwhelmed by my own hardships today, even with the blessings I have. But when I think of hers—marked by offense, loneliness, and confusion—I see a thousand deserts. All the cracks in the foundation were swallowing her alive. At one point, we lived in a friend's basement. It wasn't ideal, but it was a home; she made it one by painting a smile on her face for me and holding on with very fragile hope. Even with her tired soul and eyes, she made sure I was safe as she made a secure place for me, hoping I couldn't see how exhausted she was. I wish I could go back and tell her, "Everything is going to be okay." Instead, I get to tell you it will be more than okay. You can unmask yourself here, right now, with God. He sees it all already.

I have three beautiful children of my own now, and I am committed to healing and growing for them. In my journey, I can hear echoes of my mother's story, and I know my children will one day hear some of mine, hers, and the many stories of those who came before us—all doing the work of pulling up the weeds and letting grace take root.

This is the gift God offers: for us to walk so closely with Him that as we become more like Him, experiencing the depth of His love, we overflow with grace that touches everyone and everything around us. Little by little, we are made new. A new story is being written, and He is getting the glory for it.

I grew up understanding that home wasn't always a place but rather the people you were with. For me, Mom was home—wounds and all. Sometimes, though, our pain becomes our home too, doesn't it? My mom and I longed for stability, a life free of chaos, where brokenheartedness and disappointment didn't follow us. But isn't that what we all long for? It's how we find ourselves here, surrounded by unmet expectations—the "no," the "didn't work out," and the apologies that never came or arrived too late.

As children, we string together dreams that allow our minds to soar beyond what we could ever muster as adults. Those dreams become distant memories, mere shadows of how our thoughts once worked. Pain dims our dreaming. Visions fade, and we fade with them. We become people lost in the overgrowth, entangled in the false gods we think will save us. But they let us down, the weeds keep growing, and we wither alongside them. This is why we have to let God's grace in—if only we knew how.

Receiving God's Healing Grace

The greatest offense I have ever harbored was toward God. I struggled to comprehend how a life so full of promise could become one so consumed with pain. I used to resent feeling like a victim of my circumstances. I masked my need for God by creating distance between us and burying myself in work. I knew the words "We live in a fallen world and in the effects of it," but those words stopped being enough. Simply restating the bad news wasn't moving me forward. God wanted to show me that true freedom comes when I allow His love to free me from holding the world hostage for the wounds it could never heal.

It's His life, poured out for us, that heals us. To grow, to heal, and to love again, we must fix our eyes on what Christ has done for us—His redeeming love—more than on what tries to stain us. Jesus was asking me to focus my eyes on Him instead of the offenses, and this was my turning point.

It's His comfort that is unbroken and uninterrupted, even when we are too scared or doubtful to believe it's real. His love never wavers and never runs dry. We can be so hesitant to trust in that kind of love because we've been hurt, scarred, and weighed down by disappointment. But His love remains strong, constant, and healing. To move forward with God, we must embrace His grace over the guilt and His love over the lies. Only then can we truly grow and be healed.

Let's pause here for a moment to set some ground rules. My hope is that we can start the work of uprooting, not to criticize the past but to become aware of how we got here. Sometimes, no matter how much we plan or prepare, life throws us detours we can't explain or avoid. And instead of trying to make sense of everything, maybe the better path is to let God be God in it, bringing His goodness, comfort, power, and love to meet us where we are.

It's not about explaining the pain away; it's about taking it to Him. This is where we begin to find our way back—to peace, to healing, to Him. Letting His grace in and letting the rest go.

Your story—every twist, every wound, every offense—has shaped the person you are today. Maybe it's a single moment that changed everything or a series of small disappointments that quietly built a wall inside you. Over time, we've all tried to cope in ways that leave us feeling lost, disconnected, or unsure of who we are. If we're going to reclaim our identity, step into freedom, forgive, and live the lives we're meant for, we have to begin by acknowledging what is and allowing God to meet us there.

No amount of resentment, bitterness, or anger will change what's already happened, but surrender can change our future in it. It will be a daily act—a choice we make again and again—until the weight we've been carrying finally begins to lift. God's grace has the power to reach back and heal what we can't.

Let the Grace In

We don't want to cut the weeds. We don't love surrendering, because then who will be in the driver's seat of our lives? Even more so, who will protect our heart? We've become so accustomed to our wounds that it feels more natural to hold on than to let go. This part of our story is where we decide to face and uproot the wounds that have tied us to resentment and pain. We've turned on the light, we're seeing more clearly now through the work of the Holy Spirit, and now that we can see, it's time to let the grace in.

In Mark 5:25–34 and Luke 8:43–48, we meet a woman who has been ill for twelve years with a condition that grew worse and worse. She spent everything she had—time, money, willpower—trying to get better, only to end up stuck in the same place.

Isn't that where so many of us are at? We are desperate for healing and have exhausted every option, holding out hope that maybe this time will be the one that finally frees us.

But this woman's pain wasn't just physical. Her illness isolated her. She was considered unclean, cut off from her community, her faith, and even the possibility of marriage. If she were healed, all of that could be restored. But Jesus had more in store for her than just physical healing.

One day, she saw Jesus in the flesh. In her desperation, she thought, *If I can just touch His clothes, I'll be healed.* That thought fueled her next move. She pushed through the crowd, determined. Jesus was surrounded by people, but she reached out with a faith that went beyond proximity. She reached out with trust that He was the answer to everything she needed.

When she touched the hem of His garment, she didn't worry about the dust or what people might have thought. She simply believed. In that moment, everything changed. Jesus felt power leave His body and asked, "Who touched me?" The disciples, confused, responded, "Look at this crowd! How can You ask who touched You?" But Jesus knew this was different. Faith had met His power, and it was transformative.

The woman came forward, trembling but honest, and told Him the whole story. And then, in a moment that redefined her life, Jesus said, "Daughter, your faith has saved you. Go in peace."

That word "saved"—*sōzō* in Greek—means more than physical healing. It speaks to spiritual salvation, wholeness, and restoration. And that word "peace"—*eirēnē* in Greek—isn't just the absence of conflict. It's about harmony, well-being, and walking in step with God.

When Jesus said, "Go in peace," He was saying, "You're whole now. You're accepted. Go with me."

Can you feel the weight being lifted in those precious words? Imagine hearing them spoken over your own hurt. Take a deep breath, daughter. This is what freedom feels like.

This woman's story is about more than mere healing. It's a reminder of what happens when we surrender and our faith reaches for Jesus with everything we have. The woman's persistence and belief didn't just heal her body; they restored her identity, her place, and her peace.

Jesus didn't just fix her problem; He rewrote her story. And He can rewrite yours too:

- From the woman with the issue of blood to *daughter*
- From worthless to *worthy*
- From social outcast to *accepted and beloved*
- From anguished to *restored*

Even if the woman's condition hadn't been fully healed, that moment with Jesus changed her life forever. The Messiah had turned His attention to someone the world labeled broken, and His response was to affirm her rightful place in His family. "Daughter," He called her. Before she was anything else—before her pain, her shame, or any labels—she was *His*. The physical healing? That was just a bonus.

Healing doesn't always look the way we expect, but in Christ, it always arrives. And it's always good.

Maybe, like this woman, your journey is bringing you to surrender in ways that seem unfamiliar. Perhaps this is the moment where you go to God and say, "Take all of it, God. Cut the weeds out, uproot the lies, and free me from the bondage I've been tied to. I want healing. Help me."

I know you're tired, friend, and frustrated. I believe God is offering you an opportunity to break free, to untangle yourself from the weeds, through His power. I'm with you in it, and more importantly, our Jesus is too. I don't want you to blame yourself for how long you've sat in the enemy's trap or the way offense has kept you here for so long. Don't even go down that road—instead, let grace start flooding in. Learning to let go of offense starts with acknowledging the need to both forgive and be forgiven. When we embrace grace and see the way forward with God, the hurt that once held us hostage—along with rejection, insecurity, unforgiveness, envy, and despair—begins to fade. It's not an overnight process but a new way of believing, thinking, and living. Our beliefs impact our behavior. What we think speaks to how we live. And what we hold on to overflows as the currency of our relationships.

A Set of Traps

The work we're doing to live set free isn't about letting anyone off the hook for any wrongdoing; rather, it's about learning how to live as people loved by God. It's about becoming women who are not afraid to be wrong, to be seen, or to desperately need God.

If anything, the work of digging up the weeds and allowing God to reveal the string of offense and hurt we've carried is the work of healing and becoming—becoming more like Christ and who we are called to be in our purpose. We let go because it's how we're set free. When we let the grace in for our iniquity, we can more willingly forgive others. We all need God. Our actions do have consequences, both physical and spiritual, but ultimately, it's God who will sort all that out.

What weeds do you have in your life? What needs to be trimmed or cut down? In the Scriptures, we see the ways offense can trap us in:

- *Bitterness.* "See to it that no one falls short of the grace of God and that no bitter root grows up to cause trouble and defile many" (Heb. 12:15 NIV).

- *Unforgiveness.* "If you forgive other people when they sin against you, your heavenly Father will also forgive you. But if you do not forgive others their sins, your Father will not forgive your sins" (Matt. 6:14–15 NIV).
- *Anger.* "Get rid of all bitterness, rage and anger, brawling and slander, along with every form of malice" (Eph. 4:31 NIV).
- *Envy.* "A heart at peace gives life to the body, but envy rots the bones" (Prov. 14:30 NIV).
- *Resentment.* "'In your anger do not sin': Do not let the sun go down while you are still angry, and do not give the devil a foothold" (Eph. 4:26–27 NIV).
- *Hurt from rejection.* "Though my father and mother forsake me, the LORD will receive me" (Ps. 27:10 NIV).
- *Offense from betrayal.* "If an enemy were insulting me, I could endure it; if a foe were rising against me, I could hide. But it is you, a man like myself, my companion, my close friend, with whom I once enjoyed sweet fellowship at the house of God, as we walked about among the worshipers" (Ps. 55:12–14 NIV).
- *Hurt from words.* "The tongue has the power of life and death, and those who love it will eat its fruit" (Prov. 18:21 NIV).
- *Slander and gossip.* "A perverse person stirs up conflict, and a gossip separates close friends" (Prov. 16:28 NIV).
- *Pride.* "Pride goes before destruction, a haughty spirit before a fall" (Prov. 16:18 NIV). "Where there is strife, there is pride, but wisdom is found in those who take advice" (Prov. 13:10 NIV).

In the same way vines require oxygen from the trees and plants around them in order to grow and survive, pride takes oxygen from us—from life and all that is ahead. It is cunning and grows fast. Like the devil, pride tells us we deserve to remain angry, bitter, protective, and shut off from the world. Pride keeps the rest of the weeds feeling seen and comfortable. It tells us to stay longer in the hurt. But we know this doesn't work.

The moment we decide to allow grace in is the moment we can truly let go. It's when justifying the pain and seeking revenge or an apology can finally find end. It's the beginning of living with confidence and acceptance—accepting both who we are in Him and the life Jesus invites us to live. When we open the door to surrender, light floods in. We can't heal ourselves, but we can choose to let go with God, to forgive without forgetting, and to uproot the weeds that keep us bound. Healing comes when we let go of control, cut the weeds, and invite God in. While we learn to release the hurt, God never lets go of us.

So what's holding us hostage? It's never just one thing. We are flesh and bones, and if we don't deal with the flesh, it will deal with us. Honest, deep self-reflection is key—not only to identify the pain that needs God's healing touch but also to gain clarity on what we're up against. We can't keep playing nice with the things that are stealing life from us.

It's Time to Heal

What does healing truly mean? We hear the word everywhere, yet it often feels more like a trend than a genuine transformation we experience. Why is that? Because we're living in a generation that's deeply offended, hurt, and burned out—people searching for purpose in their pain, after the struggle, and longing for real, lasting change. Our healing journey isn't just a word—it's a path forward, guiding us through the pain toward true, lasting transformation.

The Bible offers two words that redefine healing: *sōzō* and *rapha*. Both speak to a holistic restoration. They remind us that healing isn't just about the body. It's about salvation and being made whole in every way. Sōzō gives us:

- *Spiritual salvation.* In Romans 10:9, confessing and believing in Jesus leads to being saved (sōzō).
- *Physical healing.* In Mark 5:34, Jesus tells the woman, "Daughter, your faith has made you well [sōzō]" (NKJV).
- *Complete restoration.* In Colossians 1:20, sōzō is reconciliation with God, and it also means reconciliation with others and ourselves.

Then there's *rapha*, a Hebrew word from the Old Testament that means "to heal" or "to restore." It paints a picture of God as our ultimate healer, Jehovah Rapha (Exod. 15:26). Rapha gives us:

- *Physical healing.* In Jeremiah 30:17, God says, "I will restore health to you and heal [rapha] you of your wounds" (NKJV).
- *Emotional and spiritual healing.* Psalm 147:3 promises, "He heals [rapha] the brokenhearted and binds up their wounds" (NKJV).
- *Communal healing.* In 2 Chronicles 7:14, God restores an entire nation.

Together, sōzō and rapha reveal God's heart for our wholeness—mind, spirit, body, and soul. Our true healing is about restoration, not just relief, as we pull up the weeds that choke our hearts and hand them over to God.

How's Your Heart?

Maybe your heart feels a little tender, a little more open to the idea that your future doesn't have to be tethered to offense or wounds. Imagine a version of yourself that is finally free from those weeds and living with purpose instead of pain.

As God tends to my own heart—a messy field full of tangled weeds and glimpses of beauty—I've realized something: Beneath the overgrowth is a heart that's been hidden for too long, desperate for healing. God, in His faithfulness, uncovers it layer by layer.

This process isn't without joy. Two things can be true at once: God can be mending us while we walk in victory. That's the definition of abundant life—accepting God's good gifts, abiding in Him, and living victoriously even before we feel victorious.

The weeds we pull up must go, but the uncovered heart beneath? That's where God does His best work.

Those weeds—anger, bitterness, envy, unforgiveness, pride, resentment, shame, guilt, jealousy, legalism, selfish ambition, slander, hypocrisy—have taken root. They have grown as we allowed negative emotions and sinful attitudes to fester in our hearts, leading to conflict, division, and broken relationships. They can no longer stay. Though they may be tempted to return, we will guard and work on the posture of our hearts, ensuring that they remain healthy and open to the continual tending of the One who mends and restores.

Maybe you're overwhelmed or even scared to let go of the weeds. Can I hold your hand for a moment and tell you there's no other way? It's this or a life weighed down by anger, envy, and hopelessness. A life discontented and disillusioned, where we hide behind painted smiles that no longer fool anyone, not even ourselves.

Jesus sees beyond all of it. He sees the hard heart, the quiet tears, the emotional distance, and the disconnection. Letting go isn't about pretending it didn't happen or forgetting the hurt. It's about forgiving. It's about living accepted and fully loved. And that has so much more to do with us than with the offender.

This is where we learn to exchange bitterness for hope, and anger for purpose.

What if you started to see what a life without weeds could look like? What if the very things you have been praying for are buried just beneath the pain?

Everything you hope for is on the other side of your yes to God.

When Jesus faced offense, He didn't harden His heart. He let grace in. He turned to God and leaned into truth. He loved anyway. He called people to something greater.

Tell your heart it's time to wake up. It's time to live again.

6

Step into Acceptance

It's Tuesday morning. I dropped the kids off at school, and I'm home, already sifting through emails, gearing up for a day full of meetings. As I pour my second cup of coffee, my phone buzzes with a text that instantly knots my stomach: *Hey Alex, I'd like to meet with you when you can.*

I don't talk much to this person, but when I do, it seems like it's usually about an issue. She's a friend of a friend, someone I've tried to stay cordial with—or, if I'm being honest, someone I've wanted to like me. But this message stirs up a familiar feeling. I've been here before, and I'm pretty sure I know where she stands. She doesn't seem to like me.

The last time we met, she told me I wasn't a good enough ministry leader. Not authentic enough. Not real enough. I listened, and it hurt. I tried to glean whatever good I could from the conversation, but the weight of it still lingers. And now here I am again, staring at my phone, anxiety tightening my chest.

I remember how the first time we sat down for coffee, she brought up how she had tried to connect with me years ago and how it didn't go anywhere. She admitted that it had left her feeling offended. She wasn't wrong. I hadn't pursued the connection—not out of ill intent but because I was overwhelmed, drowning in a season of life that felt all-consuming. Between kids, marriage, unresolved church hurt, and the sheer weight of daily demands, I simply didn't have the emotional capacity to give. It wasn't personal, but it left an impact all the same.

I apologized. I told her I was sorry for not communicating better where I was at. That was all I could do. Could I have overexplained myself? Sure. Could my boundaries have felt too sharp? Probably. Was I distant? Maybe. But was there ever real proximity to begin with?

There was offense on her end and insecurity on mine. The root of rejection ran deep on both sides. I'm sure what she perceived as slights from me burdened her just as much as her criticisms weighed on me. Offense hurts everyone.

The truth is, I was deeply offended, and my own insecurities only magnified the offense. Maybe it was the timing of it, maybe it was the whirlwind of chaos at our church home and community already, maybe it was how exhausted I was from all the proving and protecting I was already doing, but the offense nearly destroyed me, and I hated how much it consumed my thoughts. Why didn't this woman like me? She seemed so outwardly unhappy with who I was as a woman and a ministry leader. It felt to me like she was my biggest critic.

Offense loves to take root in the places where we're most insecure. I tried to make amends, but no amount of apologies or softness seemed to help.

It's interesting, isn't it? How much we want to *not* care. How our hearts beg for freedom from the tightrope we walk in relationships and expectations. But it seemed this woman was set in her views, her beliefs, her perceptions about me.

Sometimes we have to release people to their own ideas of truth—even if they aren't true.

There are moments when God teaches us to let go through situations we cannot control. And then there are the deeper lessons: learning to release what others have believed, spoken, and declared over us. Letting go isn't just about walking away from a situation or offense; it's about surrender. Surrendering our need to check and balance every relationship. Surrendering our need to be liked and loved by everyone. Surrendering our desire to be agreed with, understood, and accepted.

And yet, I kept asking myself, *What did I actually do to her?*

I never spoke ill of her. I never ignored her. I always acknowledged her when I saw her. But offense doesn't reason—it grows roots and strangles until it dims the light within us.

I went over every scenario in my head, searching for ways she might have been right. I spiraled into shame and people-pleasing, convinced that if I could win her acceptance, maybe it would heal my offense. Maybe it would heal hers too.

I went out of my way to say hello, to greet her kids, and show her that I wasn't everything she seemed to think I was. If I could just make her see who I really was. But none of this was motivated by a desire for an honest or fruitful friendship. It was about acceptance. It wasn't out of love but out of selfishness and pride. I was tending to my soul, making sure I did what was necessary to perform.

Offense turns into an internal battle. Unaware of our own response, we become resentful and jarred by others' words and actions, pushed to protect ourselves instead of processing the hurt. I, too, have picked up offense left and right. I have watched how others dismiss or disregard me. I have assumed rightly or wrongly and made judgments that weren't mine to make. I have walked in pride.

The truth is, letting go requires a type of confidence—safety and security that can only be found on the other side of confronting the insecurities that bubble up when offense meets us. When we are wounded and left confused about who we are, the confidence we once had escapes us like a distant memory, slowly dissolving into the shadows of our minds.

There will always be someone who makes us feel like we don't belong. But do we want to be in that relationship? Does it honor God? Does it help us grow in faith or further our calling? There will always be tables where we will never have a seat, so why do we so desperately want to sit there? Don't we believe God seats us where He wants us?

Despite our stubbornness, God offers a gracious invitation to heal the insecurities that hold us back, freeing us from the emotional chains. Walking in acceptance with God is where we can begin to live free from the burden of offense.

My Confession

I need to be honest with you—I am not naturally confident. Although what I perceived as this woman's obvious disapproval did a number on my sense of self, it wasn't the first time I had felt slighted and broken. I've waited most of my life to be invited, loved, seen, valued, and accepted.

I grew up with a mom who always told me how loved I was, even on her worst days. On days when life felt impossible for her—when depression and darkness tried to take her life—she continued to push me to a place of courage and confidence she once tried to live out in her own life. Sometimes in our wounding, it's easier to offer a vision to others of what we feel we can't attain for ourselves. My mom taught me to believe in the impossible, to hope for more, and to dream of a future, even when the world around me said otherwise. She defended me when I felt small and broken. Still, while my mom did her best to fill the gaps of my insecurities and pain, the damage of others' words had already been done.

If you were to ask me about my insecurities, I'd tell you they are attached to a string of memories—like a reel of the most embarrassing, hurtful moments of my life. Memories of rejection, letdowns, belittlement, and betrayal used to play on a loop in my mind. They were small moments in time, but those moments marked me.

Sticks and stones may break our bones, but words? Words *do* hurt us. They break parts of us that take years to mend. Words hold so much power. If I asked you to recall a time when someone made you feel less than—a moment of pain, hurt, or rejection—I'm sure you'd have a memory tied to that feeling.

"Mery, tell her to stop eating so much! She's taken so much of the dinner already!"

I already knew my body wasn't like my cousins'. I knew because it was always a topic of conversation. I was shaped more like my dad: wider, thicker, not enough curve, and too much hip. I wondered if my body would always stay the same. I wondered why I wasn't small or thin like them. I overanalyzed everyone I saw, their every glance and word sticking to me like sap on a tree. I looked down at my plate in shame, the weight of it all making my appetite disappear.

That wound took up a world of offense in my heart, and for good reason. I had no rubric for truth and lies, no framework to help me sort through who I was versus what others said about me. When we don't know who we are, we accept the stories and lies others tell us. That wound I received as a young girl turned into an eating disorder and body image issues. It turned into constant self-criticism and a feeling of fear surrounding my body. This bled into every other area of my life.

These little traps—these words we carry—hold us hostage. Weeds grow around them, and from the root of offense comes an overflow of pain. Offense will deal with us if we don't deal with it. The critical tongues, sharp words, and careless remarks of others cause more harm than they know. But here's the thing: Their behavior comes from somewhere too. When we allow God to deal gently and lovingly with *us*, His grace becomes our currency. We were never meant to live chained to offense. We were always meant to live free.

It doesn't matter how old we are, how mature we consider ourselves, or how far along we believe we are in the faith. Until we let God heal the wounds of offense, we'll experience only a shadow of peace, joy, and healing. But on the other side of surrender, there is fresh wind and new wine. We can let go, because God holds on.

Words Matter

Each of us has the capacity to carry around a world of trauma, pain, and unhealed wounds based on the words of others. These words break us, belittle us, and batter our sense of worth and value. They become grafted into our DNA, overlaying God's design and work until we start to see the world through that broken filter.

Yes, words do in fact matter, and what we believe about those words has the capacity to break us, wound us, and leave us hurt in ways we spend our whole lives working to restore. This is why our beliefs about God's words are deeply significant to Him. He knows how powerfully they shape who we are, how we live, and how we treat others. That's why He calls us to use our words with intention, and to choose words that honor Him and each other, reflect His love, and bring restoration to His people. How we speak to ourselves and others holds eternal weight, carrying the power to build His kingdom and reveal His grace.

Here are a few verses that remind us of the importance of our words and the responsibility we carry in how we use them:

> The tongue has the power of life and death,
>> and those who love it will eat its fruit. (Prov. 18:21 NIV)

> Do not let any unwholesome talk come out of your mouths, but only what is helpful for building others up according to their needs, that it may benefit those who listen. (Eph. 4:29 NIV)

> But I tell you that everyone will have to give account on the day of judgment for every empty word they have spoken. For by your words you will be acquitted, and by your words you will be condemned. (Matt. 12:36–37 NIV)

> Let your speech always be gracious, seasoned with salt, so that you may know how you should answer each person. (Col. 4:6)

Pray this prayer with me:

Dear God, I'm tired of living from a place of insecurity. I don't know where I left my confidence. My feelings are fickle, my soul is heavy, and my heart is shattered. I confess I'm carrying around offense. It's crippling me—I don't remember who I am or who I'm called to be, but I know You know. I know You remember, because You never forget. Cover my heart with Your love, God, so my wounds will be healed and my insecurities replaced with unshakable security in You. May the words once spoken over me that broke or bound me be torn down and Your Word in me lifted up. Help me remember who I am, past my wounds and hurt. Help me to lay them down and let them go. To walk in the acceptance and forgiveness only You can give. I am made to live free. This is true in You. In Jesus' name, amen.

We are letting go and regaining what we've lost, friend. I know we've lost so much. But what's ahead is a future where today's version of us exhales.

Moving On from Stuck

Most of us acknowledge only the parts of our pain that feel manageable, hoping the rest will somehow fade away. We say we've moved on, but our lives tell a different story. We struggle with broken self-worth, question God's design, and live as torn canvases. The wounds we ignore, the ones we've hidden even from ourselves, become the silent drivers of our lives. They steer our faith, emotions, and behavior, whispering lies from the back seat: "You're the sum total of your past and present.

There's no future beyond this pain, disappointment, anger, fear, or insecurity. They don't deserve to forget, so neither can you." We move through life with words that sound like forgiveness: "I've moved on. That's in the past. I'm fine." We paint a picture that we've let go of the offense. But we aren't meant to carry offense at all.

Unhealed hurt has a way of cutting deeper than we realize. And the more we leave it unsaid and unheard, the more we lose ourselves in it. Offense takes root, becoming the lens through which we see everything. It's a cycle of rejection and defeat. We live rejected and offended—not only by others but by ourselves. Sometimes we become our worst enemies too.

We reject the possibility that God could do something new. We fall into a cycle of doubt, despair, and disillusionment. But here's the truth: *We don't have to live this way.* This is the moment we turn the page.

There are three parts to this work of letting go:

1. *Trading our garment.* This step is about letting go of the person we've been—the one defined by wounds, past hurts, and everything tied to life outside of Christ's love. It's the difficult but necessary process of dying to the old self, the self that holds on to pain, shame, and past identities.

    To make this practical: Take time in prayer to consciously surrender your past hurts, identity, and fears to God. Write them down, say them out loud, and ask God to remove anything that is not aligned with His love. As you do, choose to let go of those old ways one at a time, trusting that God will make room for a new garment—one of peace, freedom, and grace.

2. *Living from love.* Living from love means no longer trying to earn or prove your worth, but choosing to live from the secure place of knowing you are loved unconditionally by God. This is where true transformation happens.

    To make this practical: Start each day by reminding yourself of God's love for you. Write out a simple declaration such as "I am loved, I am enough, and I am free in Christ." When struggles or offenses arise, pause and reflect on that truth—don't let your circumstances define you. Practice choosing love over fear or insecurity, and make it your first response to everything that challenges you. Picture yourself living *from* it.

3. *Moving beyond awareness to action.* Awareness is crucial, but transformation comes when we move beyond simply acknowledging our pain or wounds to actively stepping into the freedom God has for us.

    To make this practical: Take specific, intentional actions each day that align with who God says you are. This could mean reaching out to someone you've hurt or been hurt by, forgiving someone, or stepping into a new area of your life with confidence, even if it feels uncomfortable. Living radically means acting on what you know to be true, even when it's hard. Ask God for the courage to live out what He's calling you to, one step at a time.

How to Live Loved

How do we live loved? Deep down, we all crave security, confidence, and the abundant life God offers us. For me, it started with allowing myself to feel it all—the ache of the seven-year-old who longed to be noticed, the yearning of the young woman who rushed into love, only to face the sting of rejection again. It was in facing those moments that I began to heal.

I had to let myself sit with the weight of the woman who constantly felt overlooked and passed by. The woman who spent her life guarding her heart, bracing against the weight of disappointment. I didn't judge, didn't skip over the hard parts. I had to be honest with myself, allowing the truth of where I was to surface, even when it felt uncomfortable to confront.

But the real breakthrough came when I learned to live from a place of deep acceptance in Jesus. That's when I started trusting that I was loved—then, in the middle of all the mess, and now, no matter what life threw at me. The more I allowed that truth to sink in, the more I realized living loved wasn't just something I should know; it was something I needed to breathe in every single day. This is when my posture shifted. I began to live again.

Living loved means choosing to inhale His love and exhale His freedom, choosing every day to embrace His truth and trust that He sees me, He loves me, and He holds me through it all. Acceptance isn't just a passive thought; it's an active, daily choice to trust in who He says I am and to live fully from that place. Acceptance—allowing God's love to wash over me—moved me from being stuck in my wounds to living in peace. It prepared my heart for the inevitable offenses life will bring.

We all have a choice: to pick up the offense or lay it down. God has given us the wisdom, the power, and the authority to face whatever hurt comes our way. We don't have to stay trapped in the turmoil. We are called to live free. When we know who we are in Christ, we no longer let hurt define us. When this truth settles in, we experience the greatest change.

Yes, we've been wounded. Yes, something inside of us broke. Yes, we've been rejected and hurt by others. And yes, we might feel tender, insecure, or even defensive. But one thing is for sure: We are ready to move forward. Acceptance is the turning point. It's the key to unlocking a whole new experience of being united with Christ. It's what breaks the chains of offense we've been carrying. God gives us the grace to move on, to heal, to step into the future He's calling us to. We don't need to keep searching for someone else to define us. We're ready to believe what God says about us. Knowing who we are in Him doesn't just anchor us; it settles us deeper into His grace, and that grace is what truly sets us free.

A good question to start with is this: Do we actually know who we are? I've come up with the "right" or "good" answers to these questions—ones that perhaps make me seem more mature, intelligent, and free. But sometimes it's not enough to know the truth until we begin to live it. I'd love for us to throw away any preconceived notions about what defines us, because:

- It has little to do with the confidence we present outwardly.
- It has nothing to do with what we allow to give us our worth.
- It is not our past, present, or future circumstances.
- It was never others' acceptance or rejection of us.
- It's not the trauma or the story we've been living into.
- It's not the new role, degree, or financial freedom we've walked into.
- It's actually not merited or found in anything we could do with our human hands.

Our true identity isn't based on any of those things. Our true identity is beloved. We are each the loved-on daughter or son of Jesus, created with gentleness, intention, purpose, and power, never forgotten, and never abandoned.

We are deeply loved, and this is the truth that will carry us as we learn to find ourselves again in Christ, as we learn that preparing for future hurt requires healing from the hurt we have now. The work we do right now in practicing acceptance and living from love is what prepares us for the future offenses we will face.

Living Secure

I find myself meeting up with the same woman from church, the one who wounded me so deeply. It's been two years, and for some reason, she decided to reach out. Now we are at one of my favorite Starbucks, but my guard is up. I order my regular latte. "Hi, a grande brown sugar latte, one pump of brown sugar, please." I avoid making eye contact with her at all costs and awkwardly stare at every single Starbucks gift card and water bottle I can find. I do smile, though, because I can't glare. I'm here, and trying. But my heart is not where I want it to be. It's defensive, prickly, and on high alert. "She will not catch me off-guard again. I let her walk all over me last time," I say to myself.

It's inevitable now—we have to look at each other. I'm sitting. "Hi!" I say, trying to appear excited. We don't hug this time. We make small talk, and I dread every second of it. I'm ready to tell her how wrong she was, how much she hurt me, and how she left me confused and questioning my self-worth like I was back in middle school.

"I wanted to get together to actually apologize to you," she says, interpreting my thoughts.

She begins to tell me how, since our last conversation, she has been wanting to apologize for the bitterness and resentment she showed up with. "I placed expectations on you that weren't yours to carry," she explains.

I sigh. Haven't we all? We talk about life. I hear her heart, and she hears mine. It's a simple conversation, but so helpful. I accept her apology, and we hug.

As we part, I feel both a sense of release and an overwhelming guilt wash over me. That's when it finally clicks: We're all trying not to live from a place of woundedness, but we're not sure how to move on. We're trying to trust, but we don't know how to forgive. We're striving not to live for acceptance, yet we can't help but notice all the rejections and not yets. We're tied to the invitation and the place at the table, but we're also bound by our beliefs, ideologies, and expectations of life. And when someone lets us down, offense is the natural reaction.

She leaves first, and I have a moment to catch my breath and settle my soul. I've lived in the tension of this woman's rejection and dismissiveness for years now. I've let my soul think that some, if not all, of what she said was true. I created narratives and lived into the corresponding lies. It wasn't just with her, though. Underneath my offense is a woman who needs deep work done on her soul. I'm depleted, walking around and living from a place of insecurity.

I wonder what our lives would be like if we didn't wait for the acceptance, apology, or release before we let go of the wound. What if I hadn't waited two years for her apology to begin letting go? What if offense didn't have to control me? That coffee meetup helped me see how wrapped up I was in waiting on someone else's yes or no. How my offense was somehow dealt with when a human was able to make amends.

As I sit in that Starbucks, Jesus sits with me, the sound of the espresso machine hissing beneath the low murmur of voices around me. His presence wraps around me like a familiar song. He doesn't rush me, He just stays. And somehow, His nearness speaks louder than all the noise I've carried.

He whispers words that begin to unravel and heal all the offenses I've been carrying my entire life—the wounds that never got an apology, the grief I never knew how to name. I feel relief as I begin to see things more clearly. With a voice stronger than shame, He says, "I've made amends for you. So many amends. I love you."

A Woman to Learn From

In Matthew 15:21–28, we encounter a gentile woman who, despite every obstacle—fear of rejection, judgment, and ridicule—bravely approaches Jesus to heal her demon-possessed daughter. Her faith, fueled by love, overpowered any offense or discouragement she faced. She believed Jesus could heal her daughter, and her courage moved her to action.

Though Jesus initially ignored her and the disciples urged her to leave, the woman didn't let offense take hold. She was focused solely on one thing—Jesus as healer. Despite the barriers of culture and the risk of rejection, she persisted. Jesus recognized her great faith, and her daughter was instantly healed.

Her faith left no room for offense. Her love for God and hope in Him overcame anger, doubt, and despair. When we live anchored in the love of God and faith in Christ, offense loses its power. This woman's radical faith and acceptance show us what it means to live from a place of security in Christ, unbothered by the opinions of others. Living from love, we respond to offense as mended. When we trade our old life for the new, we live from acceptance and offense no longer defines us. This is a taste of freedom in Christ, walking in faith even when we can't see the outcome.

Turning the Corner and Living from Love

We're feeling everything now. Our hearts are tender, and God has revealed what's been keeping us bound and what's been choking us under the weight of its deadly vines. We can see how we've wrongly loved people for our own sake, how we've lived in bondage to rejection, always anxious and striving. Perhaps we have also been made aware of the ways we have offended others. But now we have the opportunity to settle into a new way forward with Jesus:

- We can choose to trust God's plans for us.
- We can believe that the work of the Spirit in others is ongoing (we don't need to control or manipulate).
- We can surrender our timeline to God.
- We can live loved, not as less than.
- We can stop living for the approval of others.
- We can stop living for affirmation from others, and instead live out of God's love for us.
- We can become more and more confident in who God has designed us to be.

When we know who we are, we live as beloved. Loved people have a perspective on life that is different. They live from a love and security so deep, it's like the roots of a tree—strong and steady, holding them firm through the fiercest storms. They're not defensive or pushy, critical or cowardly, aggressive or passive-aggressive. They're grounded and secure in who they are called to be.

Loved people are aware of the potential hurt from those around them, but they know that hurt cannot define them. They understand this truth deeply:

- Sometimes you'll be the villain in a story you can't control.
- Your story may be messy, but it is still beautifully yours.
- Healing is your responsibility—with God—and no one else's.

Loved people know that living accepted is much more powerful than living offended, understanding that we are imperfect and in process. That we are whole and loved in God.

Learning to let go of people, circumstances, and beliefs that have held us captive requires two things. I once thought only forgiveness was required, and though forgiveness is non-negotiable in our stories—and in the kingdom of God—I have realized we also must learn to live from love and acceptance. This is how we prepare for offense: living so loved by God and loving others so deeply in response that offense has nothing to hold on to it. This is the way of Jesus. If we can learn this, we can learn how to let offense go before ever picking it up.

Take Back Your Identity

It was spring break, and somehow we'd gotten away as a family for just a few days. It was a secluded area surrounded by trees that had seen more years than all of us put together. When we pulled into the driveway, everyone let out an exhale. I turned around and smiled at the kids. "We're here, guys!" I shouted.

I try not to live for getaways, but sometimes pulling away and getting alone is exactly what our souls need. We opened the door and instantly felt relief—rest was here. Our kids somehow knew exactly where their rooms were. They immediately found the bunk beds and toys downstairs. I could hear the sounds of their giggles and conversations, and they provided me with a few moments of peace in the middle of some big internal storms. We were living in a moment where joy should have been the only emotion, but I couldn't help noticing an overwhelming sense of angst creeping in right alongside it. We had gone away to rest and reset, but when offense is your travel companion, it's hard to experience life to its fullest.

Mario saw me processing, and I struggled to look at ease, because unfortunately, I wear all my emotions on my sleeve. My face said it all.

"What are you thinking about?" he asked.

"I don't want to talk about it," I said.

"You have to," he replied gently.

"It's about the women's event. It's really bothering me. I'm so tired of going over the same thing again and again. Why does everything always feel like an uphill battle? Am I the problem?" I tossed a towel into the sink.

"I know, I see you," he responded.

My church was hosting a women's event, and I wasn't asked to participate. It felt so strange. I've always been deeply involved in women's ministry. I love serving the women in our church and our community. On one level, it felt like rejection, but it went deeper than that. It felt like I was being overlooked in the very spaces where I had invested so much of myself. It seemed almost petty and prideful to feel this way, but I couldn't shake it.

I had talked to the leadership team about women's groups and events for years. I advocated for us to host gatherings, to equip women, to call them up, and to create spaces just for them. I offered to lead the women's ministry, to piece it all together, and even to pass it off—whatever it took. I helped get the ministry off the ground, organized content, and visited retreat centers. We planned and built and did two studies online during COVID, just waiting for the chance to start back up in person. But when we finally did, I heard nothing. No conversation, no transition. It was like I was never a part of the team.

One of my friends had taken it on, and she would be great at it. It was a dream for her. But if I was honest, I missed the women's ministry. I loved serving there. So I offered to lead a small group and help set up for events. I did it unto God and happily, but when I learned that a women's retreat was being planned without me, I was so hurt. It felt like the hundredth time something like this had happened.

I just couldn't make sense of it. I replayed every moment, dissecting it all. Was the leadership worried I wanted the spotlight? I never asked to speak; I just wanted to serve. Was I hurt over the lack of communication? That was part of it, definitely. But more than that, it was just . . . sticky. A strange, unresolved situation that I couldn't shake.

The whole thing could point to so many underlying issues: boundaries, insecurities—mine and theirs—confusion about roles and transitions, and so on. Relationships had grown tense. Questions about my loyalty to the ministry lingered as my commitment to both writing and speaking was often brought up. I spent days spinning, trying to prove how committed I was, how deeply invested I was. Wasn't eight years enough?

Here's the thing: This situation became a catalyst for the work I do now—figuring out why I took everything so personally—because even when there was truth in my perceptions or emotions, the problem wasn't the circumstances themselves. It was the *power* I gave the offense. I let it define me, diminish my worth, and make me question my calling. It became a trap—a stronghold.

What made the situation worse is that whenever I sensed tension or asked about it, my concerns were brushed aside. I was desperate to make sense of it all, to move forward, and to let go. But I learned the hard way that letting go can never rest in someone else's hands.

Let me pause and tell you this: Sometimes people won't address the tension or conflict you feel. They may not even acknowledge it exists. You'll have to decide for yourself if you are going to live free from the turmoil they're unwilling to resolve.

Offense comes in different ways, sometimes from your own insecurities, sometimes from the insecurities and slights of others. But whether it's handed to you or you pick it up yourself, you still have a choice. You can hold on to it or you can lay it down. And here's the truth: You can't always reconcile or resolve hurt—some human relationships will just be what they are—but you can lay it down. The real work—the healing—happens between you and God.

Mario said it best that day in the lake house when he reminded me, "You need to remember who you are in Christ—not in your emotions, their rejection, your anger, or their perception. This is where you've been stuck your whole life."

Our security, safety, and ability to show up in the world flow from one place: our identity and oneness with Jesus. When we live from that identity, we live loved and we deeply love others. Living loved changes everything.

I wasn't living loved. I didn't know how to let go of the offense or see myself apart from others' actions.

"If you were the problem," Mario said, "you're doing your best to work it out with God, me, and your friends—any blind spots you've missed. But also, two things can be true at once. You may stir something in them they don't understand, just as you need to learn how not to pick up and live from offense. Do you know who He says you are, Alex?"

Mario knew what to say. He wiped the tears from my face. It seemed I'd found my worth and identity in the wrong things. God will often allow the storms of our lives to expose what we've wrongly secured ourselves to. I heard Jesus whisper, "You are My beloved. It's time to come out from underneath the weeds."

Whether it's with my husband, family, church, or friends, discovering who I am outside of the words, opinions, slights, and perspectives of others has been the hardest work of my life. It has also given me the ability to step forward into a life of freedom.

The most powerful thing is to know the truth about God and ourselves. Learning to believe that I am who God says I am has healed my heart and restored my soul. His words are the truth that combats the lies the enemy uses to drag up past offenses, wounds, moments, words, strongholds, and anything else that once held power over me.

- *You are fearfully and wonderfully made*: "I will praise you because I have been remarkably and wondrously made. Your works are wondrous, and I know this very well" (Ps. 139:14).
- *You are of great value to God*: "Aren't two sparrows sold for a penny? Yet not one of them falls to the ground without your Father's consent. But even the hairs of your head have all been counted. So don't be afraid; you are worth more than many sparrows" (Matt. 10:29–31).
- *You are a child of God*: "See what great love the Father has given us that we should be called God's children—and we are!" (1 John 3:1).

- *You are chosen and holy:* "You are a chosen race, a royal priesthood, a holy nation, a people for his possession, so that you may proclaim the praises of the one who called you out of darkness into his marvelous light" (1 Pet. 2:9).
- *You are deeply loved:* "God proves his own love for us in that while we were still sinners, Christ died for us" (Rom. 5:8).

God's Word is both sweet and strong—comforting like honey, offering peace to my soul, and sharp like a sword, protecting and guiding me with truth. It brings clarity to my path and steadies my heart with a renewed sense of purpose.

We Are Not What We Think

Galatians 2:20 says, "I have been crucified with Christ, and I no longer live, but Christ lives in me. The life I now live in the body, I live by faith in the Son of God, who loved me and gave himself for me."

The term "union with Christ" speaks to the profound connection believers have with Jesus—a spiritual bond where our identity, purpose, and destiny are rooted in Him. His life, death, and resurrection shape our own transformation. It's about discovering our true self and meaning in Him.

The idea of union with Christ came alive for me during one of the most impactful therapy sessions of my life. My counselor helped me unpack my shattered identity and distorted view of myself and God.

Letting go requires what I call "identity work"—learning to live apart from others' approval and even our own expectations.

It means living securely in Christ's acceptance. All who believe in Him are gifted the grace of becoming God's children (John 1:12), permanently loved and held by the Father, since nothing can separate us from His love (Rom. 8:38–39). The more secure we are in Christ, the less insecurity has power over us.

Imagine a canvas, pristine and full of potential, stretched across a frame, ready to display a beautiful masterpiece. The artist, with great care and intention, begins to paint a stunning image, rich with color and detail. Each brushstroke adds depth, meaning, and purpose, reflecting the unique design intended for the canvas.

However, over time, the canvas is torn and slashed. The once-vibrant colors become obscured by deep gashes, and the masterpiece is left incomplete, marred by damage. What was meant to be a beautiful expression of identity and purpose now appears broken and unfinished. This torn canvas represents a soul scarred by life's challenges, haunted by self-doubt, and burdened by a sense of worthlessness. It reflects someone shaped by the false narratives they've believed about who they are, each tear and fray echoing the wounds of their inner battle.

Friend, this torn canvas represents the distortion of how we see ourselves. God, the Master Artist, has created each of us with a unique design, purpose, and identity in Christ. He has woven into our being a reflection of His image, a masterpiece that is meant to display His glory, love, and grace.

But the enemy seeks to tear and distort that image. Through lies, fear, and experiences that undermine our worth, the canvas of our souls can become damaged. We may see ourselves as unworthy, inadequate, or beyond repair. The vibrant colors of our identity in Christ may seem dull and lifeless, obscured by the wounds we've endured.

Yet the torn canvas does not define our worth or our future. In Christ, we are not left broken and unfinished. Jesus, the Redeemer, steps in as the restorer of our souls. He takes the torn canvas of our lives and begins the work of mending, healing, and restoring it to its intended beauty.

Through His grace, He carefully stitches the tears, blends the colors, and completes the masterpiece that He always intended. The scars remain, but they become part of the story and a testimony of His love and redemption. What was once a source of shame and brokenness is transformed into a display of His power to heal and restore.

In Christ, our identity is not determined by the damage we've experienced but by the hands of the One who holds us. He sees the masterpiece within us even when we cannot. He calls us His own, beloved and cherished, regardless of the tears in our canvas. Our worth is found not in our perfection but in His love and the identity He has given us as His children.

So, while the torn canvas may represent the struggles we face with self-worth and confidence, it also holds a promise. In Christ, we are being made whole and our identity is secure. The Master Artist is not finished with us yet, and the masterpiece He is creating will reflect His glory in ways we may not yet see.

A New You

There's a new me on the horizon. I can see a glimpse of what Christ has promised: a woman who can live loved and secure, with a purpose and boldness that aren't rooted in human prediction or satisfaction, that can't be given or taken away. My heart is learning that I am safe and loved because I am found in

Christ. I am safe and loved because I no longer have to live by the words or opinions of others. I can more freely love and let people fail, including myself. It's scary, yes, but learning to let go means learning to let God be God in my life and everyone else's. I am not ultimately in control. God is.

I've found it hard to carry offense the more I know how loved and secure I am. I've found it hard to be brittle and bruised and critical toward those who have wounded me, and easier to be soft and gracious to those I have wounded too. Love reveals, but it does not harden. Love reveals, but it does not condemn. It invites us into deeper grace, it softens the edges of our hearts, it offers a way forward with kindness. This is Christ in us, as we learn to let go for our good and His incredible glory. And we need His Spirit in us, His power, and His miraculous work, because we know that in our flesh and in our woundedness we have tried on our own and failed. And it's okay. It's okay that we've not been able to accomplish this freedom on our own, because we were always meant to do it through His power.

Paul understood this tension, as much of his ministry was spent teaching the people of God all about their new identity. In an effort to encourage the believers in Ephesus, a city in Asia Minor, Paul wrote to them, urging them to embrace their new identity in Christ. He reminded them of the importance of walking in their "new self," throwing off their sinful ways and putting on the righteousness and holiness they had received in Jesus (Eph. 4:22–24). Paul knew they would be tempted to return to their old patterns of thinking and behaving—living divided, selfish lives shaped by their past. But he called them to something higher: to be transformed by the renewing of their minds, to live in unity, and to let go of the old, corrupt self.

This transformation is possible only through the Spirit's power and is a testimony to God's incredible grace. Through Christ *in us*, this is the miracle: to let go and let Him do it. It's all His power and work, even in our weakness, our less than, our not enough.

I've often struggled to see beyond the various identities I've adopted throughout my life. They have become so ingrained in me that they feel like an inescapable part of who I am. Perhaps you can relate. We often live according to the identities shaped by our wounds, the roles we've been assigned, or the ones we've crafted for ourselves. Here are some examples of these identities and how offense can subtly shape and reinforce them:

1. *The wounded protector.* This identity arises from a sense of being hurt or betrayed in the past, often leading to a hypervigilant stance to avoid further pain. When operating from this identity, we may hold on to offense as a way to protect ourselves from future wounds, seeing every slight or criticism as a potential threat. This lens is one of self-defense and self-preservation, making it hard to let go of offenses because the hurt has become a shield.

    The new you. In Christ, we can recognize how living from a place of fear and self-protection distances us from the safety and security we already have in Him. Holding on to offense is often about protecting a wound that Jesus longs to heal. His love is our true shield.

2. *The justice seeker.* This identity holds tightly to a sense of right and wrong, and we often feel compelled to correct injustices or wrongs done to us or others. Offense becomes a tool to demand justice or fairness. This lens

is one of moral rightness, where we see the world in stark terms of offense and defense.

The new you. In Christ, we learn that true justice is not ours to enforce but God's to administer. Holding on to offense in the name of justice can blind us to His deeper work of mercy, grace, and reconciliation. When we release our grip on offense, we entrust ourselves to God's sovereignty, understanding that His justice is perfect and His ways are higher than ours. His righteousness, not our sense of moral rightness, becomes our foundation.

3. *The overcomer.* This identity is centered on resilience and strength, often shaped by past struggles or adversity. When we see ourselves as overcomers, we may hold on to offenses as proof of our endurance or as a way to validate our suffering. This lens is one of self-sufficiency, where strength is measured by how much we can withstand rather than by resting in Christ's strength.

   The new you. In Christ, true overcoming is not about holding on to wounds or offenses to prove our strength. It's about recognizing that His grace is sufficient for us and that His power is made perfect in our weakness. We don't have to validate our suffering or endurance by clinging to past hurts; instead, we can lay them down and find true freedom in His love. Real strength is shown in humility and surrender, trusting that Christ is our victory.

4. *The invisible one.* This identity comes from a place of feeling unseen or unheard, leading to a deep sensitivity

to perceived slights or offenses. When we see ourselves as invisible, we may hold on to offenses as proof that we are being overlooked or dismissed. This lens is one of rejection and insecurity, where every interaction is filtered through the fear of being ignored or devalued.

The new you. In Christ, we are fully seen, known, and loved. Our identity is defined not by how others perceive or acknowledge us but by the truth that God delights in us and calls us His own. When we let go of offense, we release the need for human validation and rest in the assurance that we are valued and cherished by God. His love is enough to fill every void, and His gaze never leaves us.

5. *The pleaser.* This identity is rooted in a need to be liked, accepted, or validated by others. When we identify as pleasers, we may either internalize offense, turning it into self-blame, or hold on to it as resentment toward those who did not approve. This lens is one of conditional worth, based on the fluctuating opinions of others.

   The new you. In Christ, we find a love that is unconditional and unchanging. Our worth is dependent not on others' approval but on the finished work of Jesus. We are free to live authentically, without fear of rejection or disapproval. Letting go of offense means releasing ourselves from the bondage of people-pleasing and stepping into the freedom of knowing that we are already fully accepted and loved by God.

6. *The competitor.* This identity sees life as a series of comparisons and competitions. When we view

ourselves as competitors, we often take offense when someone else seems to be winning or excelling, or when criticism is perceived as a direct threat to our standing. This lens is one of scarcity and rivalry, where offense becomes a response to perceived loss or unfairness.

The new you. In Christ, we learn that our value is determined not by earthly competition but by our eternal identity as children of God. There is no need to compare or compete when we understand that God's love for us is unique and abundant. Letting go of offense allows us to celebrate others' successes without feeling diminished and to rest in the assurance that God's blessings are infinite and tailored for each of us.

These are just a few examples of the identities we pick up and live into based on the stories of our lives. We can so easily become them, and unfortunately, they then become the very distorted lens from which we see life as we grow critical, sad, dismissive, distrusting, and discouraged.

Perhaps you were able to relate to one or more of these identities. You're safe to admit it here, between just you and God. You're tired of living this way, in insecurity, always offended, angry. And even if some of the pain is self-inflicted, you don't deserve to live in the prison of offense. It's a barrier to experiencing the fullness of life in Christ that you are both given and promised.

I am not willing to forsake the gift of security and safety in Christ for the mere scraps of human approval. I've done it for far too long and know what a life without His abundance feels like—full of strife, heaviness, and hurt. I refuse to live a life consumed by anger, a critical spirit, or pride. I've seen the damage it causes—how it leads only to more bitterness and takes away from the freedom I could have. I am not walking on the eggshells of others' expectations, unhealed wounds, or lack of self-control or self-awareness; with God I am learning to respond rightly to past, present, and future offenses. And when I feel the itch to chase approval again, to pick up old offenses, or to let bitterness take root, it's a gentle reminder that I've forgotten who I am—and whose I am.

The Life I Now Live

Paul says the essence of the Christian faith is to live crucified with Christ. Our old life no longer lives, but Christ lives in us. Our old ways are dying, and our new identity in Christ is finding its way in the midst of the old flesh. And yet, even in the face of offense, we are called to live into this new identity. Galatians 2:20 declares, "I have been crucified with Christ, and I no longer live, but Christ lives in me. The life I now live in the body, I live by faith in the Son of God, who loved me and gave himself for me."

When we come to faith, our old self—the one defined by sin, hurt, pride, and the world's standards—is put to death with Christ on the cross. This is more than a spiritual concept; it's a reality that reshapes our identity. We are no longer driven by past mistakes, wounds, or the opinions of others. Our true identity is found in Jesus. He lives in us, transforming us from the inside out.

But why does this matter when we're dealing with offense? Because offense is one of the quickest ways to drag us back into living like our old selves. It stirs up our pride, inflames our hurt, and invites us to hold on to the wrongs done to us. Offense pushes us to build walls, hold grudges, and seek revenge. But if we truly understand that we've been crucified with Christ, then offense no longer has the same grip on us.

When Christ lives in us, His love, grace, and humility become the source of our identity, replacing our pain and need for justice. Knowing this transforms how we respond to offense. Instead of reacting from a place of woundedness or defensiveness, we can respond with the confidence of knowing who we are in Him. We are not defined by the wrongs done to us or our reactions to them. Our identity is secure in Christ, who loved us and gave Himself for us, even when we didn't deserve it. To know we belong to God is to live as His.

Yet I can't help but feel that many of us are not living as though we belong to Him. Instead, we live bound by the opinions and influences of the world around us. We get tangled up in our pain, and the enemy knows just how to keep us trapped in those weeds. He wraps the vines of lies and hurts so tightly around us that we lose sight of who we truly are. We know our pain more intimately than we know our God. And I wonder, friend, is this a wake-up call for our souls? Offense is often a symptom of a deeper issue: We are living as if we are not loved by God.

I believe offense is so rampant because we have become our own gods, obsessed with wanting to be loved by others, missing the love that God has always freely given. When our sense of self is tied to the ever-changing opinions of others rather than the unchanging truth of Christ, we find ourselves lost and disappointed.

When offense comes knocking—and it will—we have a choice. We can either step back into our old selves, living out of anger and bitterness, or we can lean into the new life Christ has given us, where offense loses its grip. Offense wants to keep us trapped in the past, but our new identity in Christ sets us free to live in peace, love, and strength.

Knowing this truth—that Christ is alive in us—is crucial when dealing with offense. It reminds us that our identity is not dictated by our hurts or the actions of others but by the One who loved us enough to die for us. And that truth sets us free to move forward, unburdened by the weight of offense, and to be fully alive in our new identity in Him.

Our Identity in Christ

How we handle hurt, offense, and conflict changes everything—especially when we're secure in who we are. When we know who we are in Christ, our response is different:

- We're less focused on proving a point and more focused on letting God work in us and the people around us.
- We're willing to walk away from a situation, knowing that our identity isn't tied to the outcome.
- We don't let our worth or values get compromised, because we're confident in who we are.

When we're living from that deep, crucified self—in Christ—it changes how we love:

- We choose love over hate, forgiveness over holding on to offense.

- We commit to being self-aware and laying down our pride every single day.
- We walk the way Jesus walked—grace filled, humble, and secure in who we are.

For a very long time, I was the type of woman most likely to struggle with a crisis of identity. I didn't want to be swayed by the opinions, actions, or words of others, yet I found myself constantly seeking validation from people. This led only to insecurity. I didn't want to carry offense with me, but it became a natural part of who I was for far too long. My pain and wounds became my guiding force, my compass, leading me into seasons of confusion and doubt. I spoke and lived from a place of hurt, both old and new.

Identity is our breath, our bones, the bodies we walk in, the lives we live, the souls we steward—woven into a story that speaks volumes to the world. We are strong, weak, broken, beautiful. We are mothers, daughters, sisters, friends. We wound, we heal, we are imperfect and in process. We are not the sum of our lives but the pieces of it. We are God's creation, deeply loved. We spend our lives waiting for someone to tell us who we are. Parents choose our names, hoping they'll carry weight, meaning, and purpose. But as we grow, we realize true identity isn't handed to us from the outside; it's discovered from within. It's a journey of uncovering who we are—beyond the labels, the expectations, the roles—and finding the essence God has already written into us.

Knowing who we are in Him dismantles the need for justice in our hurts. Letting go of the right to be offended, to hold on to the wrongs done to us, is one of the hardest things we'll do. But in surrendering, we find a peace that transcends our wounds. It's a peace that comes from resting in our true identity in Christ. We are not defined by our past pains or the successes we chase. We are not what we wear or how many people follow us. We are not the judgments of others or the roles we play. Our worth is not in what we do but in who we are. We are beings first; we are not what we accomplish. Our stories shape us, but they don't define us.

Freedom comes in letting go, shedding the layers and walls we've built. True identity is like the air we breathe—it's the beginning of a full life with Christ. It's the green light to step into the life He has dreamed for us. Yet, I'll admit, living it out is challenging, especially when defeat or past hurts hold us back.

So what do we do with this new identity? We step into freedom, moving beyond the defeat that still lingers, leaving behind what has held us down. Embracing this identity isn't a onetime moment; it's a journey. This is the life we're fighting for—once stolen by the enemy, but now found again. We're stepping out of the weeds, into the light, into purpose. And the best part?

There is so much more ahead.

Move Forward with God

Move Beyond Defeat

For much of my life, I felt defeated, constantly chasing a peace and safety that always seemed just out of reach.

I held on to whatever strength I had left, simply trying to show up, while letting others shape my path. I feared disturbing the status quo, all while pretending to be strong, afraid to acknowledge the vulnerability that was just beneath the surface. But my strength was just a front—a hollow act behind my 5'3" frame. I was deeply insecure, desperately trying to hold on to people who were slipping away.

When you live in a state of defeat—feeling rejected, overlooked, and left behind—you find yourself swinging between two extremes: a relentless need for control (a hollow grasp for authority) and the exhausting performance of people-pleasing. Both lead to the same end: a life marked by emptiness and insecurity.

Living defensively gives you the illusion of control. You think that if you can keep disappointments at arm's length and people who could hurt you even farther away, you'll be safe. But in reality, you end up building walls so high that those who once felt like friends now seem like strangers—they just happen to know your name. You tell yourself that if you make life fail-proof, guarding against every offense and keeping everyone at a distance, you won't be hurt again. But that's not how it works. Instead, your heart hardens, and in trying so hard to protect yourself, you lose yourself. Defeat traps you in a cycle where letting go of the past hurts feels impossible. And then, in the middle of a completely ordinary day, it all surfaces.

For me, it was a typical workday, packed with back-to-back meetings, the juggling act of being a mom, and trying to be a decent leader to my team. Kingston, my son, was with me that day because of a doctor appointment. I sat in the waiting room, watching him play, and my mind was racing—not just about the germs I was obsessing over from the toys, but about my calendar, my responsibilities, and the weight of unseen eyes judging my every move.

Years of giving people too much say over my identity had left me living rigid, cold, and anxious. I was more defeated, less in love with life and God, less hungry to live on mission for His kingdom and people, less eager to live a life full of purpose and passion. I had granted people power they were never meant to have. I was living from a place of brokenness, trying to control how others perceived me, control my way through life, heal my own wounds, protect myself from any future ones, and keep moving forward somehow. But this only left me more irritable, less free, and hypersensitive to everyone's reactions. I lived and died by their acceptance. And we know what happens when we live and die by the words and opinions of others—we wither away too.

I was trying to juggle the responsibilities I'd been given to steward. But my soul was heavy—I was overthinking what my team would think about my absence, what my boss would say about me having to bring Kingston in. Mario had a full day of appointments that he just couldn't reschedule. We were making it work; we did what we could with what we had. My family is so blessed to have the flexibility we have, but the pressures of life often mask even the greatest of blessings if we're not careful. Sometimes we miss the blessings that are because of the pain that is.

Fear had its grip on me, tightening around my chest, whispering that I wasn't enough—at home, at work, and even in my own heart. It felt like I was always falling short, like I was living in a constant state of not enough. No matter how much I tried to give, to show up, to do my best, it never seemed to be enough for anyone else. And the worst part? It never felt like it was enough for me either. The more I tried to manage it all, the tighter the grip of fear became, leaving me paralyzed, unable to breathe easy. Would I ever be enough? Would I ever get it all right? The pressure was suffocating. I was walking on eggshells, afraid that at any moment, something would tip me over. A mistake, a misstep, one wrong word—and the delicate balance I was desperately trying to hold on to would shatter. I felt like I was drowning in my own effort, trying to be everything to everyone, and yet I was losing sight of the one person I needed to be most—myself. In the chaos of trying to meet expectations, I couldn't even hear my own voice anymore. Would I ever be able to step out of this cycle and breathe freely again?

Kingston, as always, was a trouper. He climbed into the car with his backpack, packed with everything he needed to stay busy while I worked—his book, his sketch pad, snacks, a fully charged iPad, and his favorite blanket. But no matter how much I tried to focus on the task at hand, the tightness in my chest wouldn't go away. As I tried to balance being a mom and a leader, the fear and anxiety clung to me. The fear of not being enough, of not being understood, of never measuring up. How did I get here?

Finding Our True Identity

We were almost finished with Kingston's doctor appointment, and I could still feel it. The constant fear of future wounds loomed over me like a shadow, always present, always whispering that the next hurt was just around the corner. I'd tried to shake it the whole time, to no avail. My whole life revolved around protecting myself from pain—protecting myself from the offense I was constantly living in, from what others might think of me, from whether they would accept or reject me, and from what they might say behind my back. I couldn't let my guard down; the thought of opening myself up only to be hurt again was too overwhelming. Every relationship, every interaction became a potential source of pain, and I found myself bracing for the next blow, constantly on edge. Instead of living freely or fully, I was just surviving, trying to shield myself from the next offense, the next rejection, doing everything I could to avoid the hurt that felt inevitable.

Later that day, I was driving my kids to a friend's house. Kingston was beside me in the front seat, tired from a day of activities, while my two daughters rested quietly in the back. I reached over to gently touch my son's face as he slept, feeling the exhaustion in both our souls. I had lost my footing in life, feeling disoriented, depleted, and just done. I felt a rare invitation to breathe as we drove down a quiet road lined with farms. There was no hustle, no noise, no people—just us, the farm animals, beautiful spotted cows, and the open road. I took a deep breath, trying to calm my racing heart and settle my weary soul. When did everything start to feel so heavy?

When we live from a place of offense and fear, always on guard and waiting for the next hurt to come, we end up spending our entire lives—minds, bodies, and souls—working overtime to protect ourselves from more pain. We take on a defensive role, constantly bracing for the next blow. Defeat becomes our way of life as we forfeit our joy, peace, and courage.

It was at this moment that I noticed time slowed down, and the wind blowing in my face felt like a sweet embrace from God. I exhaled. Maybe the weight I was carrying could be put down. Kingston looked up at me and smiled, as if he'd not seen this side of his mom in a long time: gentle and less hurried, anxious, and angry. I felt God's gentle whisper: "Learn to love again." This simple yet heartbreaking reminder came over me like torrential rain. My kids needed my affection, and I could perceive that perhaps the hurt of life, and the little but multiplying offenses, had consumed every bit of me. We become what we do not heal. In fact, I'd lost much of my gentleness in the last year.

We stopped at a traffic light, and I looked in the rearview mirror. I tried to see the woman with the gentleness I once remembered. She was in there, somewhere. I'd remained soft for so long—until I didn't, until I wasn't. My smile had faded. The pain in my eyes was obvious. I knew there had to be a way out.

The world I'd navigated for thirty-two years had left me bruised, with each hit hardening my heart, and every wall and barrier I'd put up to protect myself, a failure. I felt like I couldn't trust anyone. I didn't want to trust anyone. I couldn't risk anyone hurting me again. I didn't want to be strong anymore, and I also couldn't stand the thought of being weak.

Offense drives a wedge between who we are and who God calls us to be, and this is what brought me here. It calls us to callousness and hard hearts, to short tempers and critical spirits. It calls us to insecurity and gossip. It calls us to anger and bitterness. It's a virus that we cannot see, robbing us of the gift that is God's great love for us. It traps us in a cycle of defensiveness, making us believe we have to guard ourselves constantly. But that is not our true north. Disappointment doesn't have to derail us. Rejection doesn't have to paralyze us. Betrayal doesn't get to bury us. We are invited to live loved—to love deeply because we are deeply loved by God.

When we finally arrived at my friend's house, she opened the door and could immediately tell I'd been crying. Her embrace was so quick, I barely got through the doorway. "Come in," she said gently, then called over my shoulder, "Kids, go play in the backyard." We settled down outside, and the tears just kept coming. I felt like I was drowning because I didn't know how to let go.

It wasn't just one thing—it was everything. It was my dad choosing a different family and me living with the subconscious belief that I've always been second-best. It was feeling invisible as a leader at work, no matter how hard I tried to prove my capacity and ability. It was the chaos of my childhood, constantly crashing up against what seemed to me to be Mario's picture-perfect, Disney-like upbringing. It was the friendships that were weird and full of strife, the church drama, the toxic bosses, and the abuse of power. It was the sinking feeling that plagued me of never being enough for Mario or anyone else in my life. Ever.

I felt like I was always on the outside, never invited in, always having to push my way through. Every step felt like a struggle, with my every move under a microscope, being dissected and picked apart by people who never cared to truly know me. I was exhausted from the weight of it all—the need to prove myself worthy to people who seemed determined to keep me small. I felt like I was constantly fighting for a place I was never meant to belong to, trying to fit into spaces that were too tight, too cold, and too confining for the fullness of who I was created to be. I was tired of walking around feeling offended and insecure, of swinging between not caring at all and being overwhelmed by every little thing. One moment, I'd feel strong and almost defiant, and the next, I'd be crushed by a single glance or word, wondering what everyone thought of me.

I was done. Done with the striving, done with the pretending, done with feeling like I had to earn every bit of love and acceptance in my life. My heart was raw, my spirit depleted. I longed for the freedom to finally let everything fall apart and to discover a new way to be.

I knew I needed to move on, but where would I even start? It seemed clear that taking back the narrative had to be the first step. I needed to start taking "every thought captive to obey Christ," as 2 Corinthians 10:5 describes. I was not a victim of my life. I had the power to make changes, to break free and break through. Living as a powerless, defeated woman, with counterfeit versions of God's goodness and abundance, was not the answer. I needed to make changes in my life. I needed to fight for myself by letting go.

Many of us find ourselves standing at the crossroads of our new identity in Christ, feeling the weight of past defeats still lingering in our hearts. It's one thing to understand and embrace who we are in Him, but it's another entirely to live out this truth amid the remnants of old hurts and struggles. We're wedged in the middle of the new life we've been given and the old way of living. We know our identity in Christ but still feel trapped by the shadows of past failures, betrayals, and disappointments. Our journey to freedom won't be immediate, but it will begin with a single, courageous step forward.

Elijah's Moment

In 1 Kings 18:36–39, Elijah experienced something many of us can only dream of. He stood on Mount Carmel, boldly calling down fire from heaven, and the people witnessed God's power in a way that could not be ignored. It was a moment of undeniable victory. Elijah must have felt on top of the world—like a spiritual champion. But then came Queen Jezebel's threat. She swore to kill him, and just like that, everything changed. Fear and exhaustion crept in, and Elijah, who had just witnessed such a mighty move of God, ran for his life. Overcome, he wished for death (19:1–10).

This wasn't a lack of faith; Elijah's desperation actually revealed his deep dependence on God. In his lowest moment, he still turned to God with his pain—honestly, vulnerably, and without pretending to be strong. What stands out here is not just his fear but how quickly his insecurities resurfaced. Even in the face of victory, he became overwhelmed by feelings of inadequacy and fear. When we're exhausted and gripped by fear, it's easy to forget our worth and our purpose—and hard to know how to move on from the pain of the past. Just like we so often do, Elijah wondered if God had left him, if he was still worthy of his calling, and he felt incredibly alone.

Elijah had seen God move. He had been in God's presence, yet somehow, in that moment, he let fear and insecurity take over. He got so caught up in his emotions and doubts that he lost sight of everything God had already shown him. It's easy to fall back into old patterns, especially when we are overwhelmed. But even then, God didn't leave Elijah. He met him right there, with compassion, just like He does for us. Then He asked a simple yet profound question: "What are you doing here, Elijah?" (v. 9). God wasn't seeking information, nor was He confused. He already knew the answer. Instead, He was inviting Elijah to reflect on and examine where his own heart had wandered. After Elijah rested and ate, God spoke to him again—not in the wind or the fire but in the quiet. He gave Elijah new tasks, gently restoring his confidence and reminding him of his purpose. Elijah's journey wasn't over, and neither is ours.

God asks us the same gentle questions in our insecurity and pain: *Why are you hiding? What are you believing?* His voice doesn't always come in loud or dramatic ways. More often, it's a still, quiet whisper, calling us out of fear, drawing us back to truth and freedom, and reminding us of His unwavering presence. Just as He reassured Elijah, God reminds us that we're never truly alone.

We all face moments like Elijah's where defeat, exhaustion, and pain make us want to give up. But those moments don't define us. When we feel like we can't go on, Jesus meets us there, whispering hope and reminding us that there is so much more ahead. The enemy may try to steal, kill, and destroy, but Jesus came so we could have life, and have it abundantly (John 10:10).

Maybe you've had those moments, like I have, where you look back and hardly recognize yourself. Maybe you've felt that the person you were just days ago is now a stranger. I can only imagine the weight of Elijah's despair, but I know how it feels when life knocks the wind out of you so hard that moving forward—let alone with confidence or peace—seems impossible.

Where are you right now? Is it time to remember who you are? To listen for that still, small voice calling you back to life, back to hope, and back to Him?

When Life Feels Unbearable

It's 10:30 p.m., and my leather couch feels cold beneath me. I pull the throw blanket around my shoulders and open my laptop. Today has been full of coffee dates, meetings, and listening to people's lives, their struggles, and their dreams. It's a privilege, really, to be a part of it all and to hold space for others. But as I listened, I couldn't help but notice how much of their pain mirrored my own. I understand the wounds, the frustrations, and the questions that don't seem to have answers. I've lived with that secret too—the one where offense becomes a habit and letting go feels like losing the last thing holding me together.

Carrying responsibility doesn't remove you from the rawness of humanity; if anything, it amplifies it. Walking with others through their pain doesn't make you immune to your own. As I sit here reflecting on everything, I see how much I, too, have struggled. There are moments when I look at my own life and wonder if I'm truly living or just going through the motions. I turn to Jesus, asking how He would've walked through all of this. What would He do? And won't He carry me through? Won't He carry us all?

Life often feels like an unsolvable puzzle, and it's easy to feel lost in the chaos. But the one thing that holds us steady is knowing that we have God and He has us. Even when our souls are unsettled and peace seems like a distant dream, we can hold on to that truth. We wrestle with insecurities about friendships, roles, and our worth. We ask ourselves if we'll ever truly belong, be seen, or feel valued. We long for connection, for affirmation, and for love. We struggle to accept the stories we're living, to see the beauty and purpose in the pain.

But here's the thing: Moving forward requires change. Radical change. It means choosing to release what's weighing us down and pick up what we were always meant to carry: our peace, our joy, our wholeness in Christ. It means letting go of the offense, the bitterness, and the wounds that don't define us. Each of us has the choice to let go, to live fully loved by Him, and to move forward in freedom, grace, and peace.

The holdup for many of us is that, too often, we think God is like us. That perhaps He has grown distant or uninterested. We don't know Him all that well. If we don't truly believe we're forgiven and loved, it's easy to stay stuck in offense and insecurity. But when we let God's grace in—when we let it change us, soften us, and heal us—that's when true freedom begins. And it's in that freedom that we start to let go, to heal, and to embrace life as we were always meant to.

Say It Out Loud

Perhaps you've heard that saying our emotions, thoughts, and feelings out loud, or even writing them down, can help us process the hurt and offense of our lives. Doing this is supposed to move us forward, as our thoughts, emotions, and beliefs are identified and verbalized. Although this is helpful and true, a lot of what still keeps us bound up, even when we try to wrestle our emotions out, is a lack of true confession and surrender.

I can't overstate how important this is—to say out loud when we are, in fact, stuck in our offense. Confessing to God our dissatisfaction with life and our deep need for Him is a crucial step—confessing our sin and anger, our jealousy and bitterness, our unforgiveness and discontentment, our disappointment and disillusion all to Him. God can take it all for us. He can hear it, handle it, and hand us a much lighter cup than the one we've been carrying.

Confession is showing God we are done doing it our own way. Repentance is walking out the conviction of our confession. Learning to let go of offense and moving forward in our lives is much more than overlooking an offense; it's about looking up to the One who can help us live genuinely unoffendable lives.

Offense is a trapdoor, and confessing our offense is undoubtedly the first spiritual and physical step we can take toward healing. When we confess with our mouths and surrender in our hearts the offense we've been carrying, we're met with a love like no other, a comfort like no other—a God who understands what it feels like to be rejected, misunderstood, and talked down to. He knows what it means to feel righteous indignation, to both be God and also be treated like a human, as if our breath and bones and bodies weren't spoken into existence by Him. Our God, who created us, watches over creation as we carry offense toward Him and others, while He extends His hands in grace and more grace, saying, "Come in. I love you. It's time to let it go."

Pray this with me:

God, I confess that I have been carrying a weight I was never meant to carry. Offense and hurt have plagued me, and I'm tired of living a life full of anger, bitterness, and distrust. I am done living stuck in perpetual defeat. Lord, help me today to move on, to move forward, to let go, to see You, and to let You give me a new perspective, new hope, new belief, new joy, new peace, new purpose, new vision, and the courage to live out my true identity in You. Help me to live loved and love again. You are good, I love You, and I thank You, Jesus. In Your holy name, amen.

Stepping into Freedom

Stepping into freedom is more than leaving behind the wounds of the past; it's stepping into the full, abundant life that Christ offers, a life marked by peace, joy, and the certainty of being loved. This freedom calls us to move beyond survival mode, to live without fear or scarcity, and to embrace a new way of seeing ourselves and others through the lens of God's grace. Stepping into freedom means choosing a life shaped by grace and healing, not by the wounds of the past. This freedom is not a distant dream but a tangible reality waiting for us to claim. It's about breaking free from the chains of past defeats and stepping boldly into the abundant life God has prepared for us.

I want us to break free from living in the past, where insecurities or fears of never being fully loved or of being hurt again hold us back from moving forward. I don't want us to miss experiencing the freedom and peace that comes with living as Paul says, as "a new creation" (2 Cor. 5:17), created for good works and good things, to love and live loved by God.

Friends, family members, strangers, and coworkers will offend us; people will betray us; our friends will let us down, and our family will too. We will have to let some people go and choose to fight for others (in health). In all of that, we will still miss the mark, but hopefully we will humbly and gracefully realize we were all in desperate need of God every time.

True freedom from defeat and offense doesn't stop here. To walk fully in this new life, we must confront the weight that holds us back: unforgiveness. Earlier, we talked about the two-sided coin of letting go of offense:

1. learning to live loved
2. forgiveness

Forgiveness isn't something that just happens to us; it's an active choice, a deliberate act of releasing what was never ours to carry. It's not passive surrender but rather an intentional decision to lay down the weight of the hurt, the offense, and our resentment. Forgiveness isn't about excusing what was done or minimizing the pain; it's about choosing freedom over the burden of holding on.

It's a nonnegotiable if we're going to walk in true freedom and love. It takes courage, the kind of courage that doesn't wait for everything to make sense before we take a step forward. It takes surrender, releasing our grip on what has held us captive. And it takes a profound trust in the One who has already forgiven us all and shown us grace even when we didn't deserve it.

Forgiveness means letting go of the hurt, not just from others but from ourselves too. It means forgiving others—and forgiving ourselves for holding on to the wounds that were never meant to define us.

It was the moment I realized freedom couldn't come without forgiveness that I knew I could truly begin to let go of offense once and for all. And in that moment, I chose to step into the kind of freedom that comes only from laying it all down.

Figuring Out Forgiveness

> To forgive is to set a prisoner free and discover that the prisoner was you.
>
> —Lewis B. Smedes

"The gift is not like the trespass" (Rom. 5:15). The words from this verse echoed in my heart like a soft melody, and I couldn't help but linger over them during an evening devotional with my oldest daughter. I'd never read the passage like I did that day. The week's theme was forgiveness. As I sat on the edge of her bed, reading Romans 5:15–17, I felt an old, familiar tension loosening its grip on me. Tears welled up as I tried to get through the devotional. Something was stirring. I kissed my girl good night and tried to hide the tears waiting to let loose.

Our tears tell stories. They water the soil for growth beneath us, and we must let them come.

I walked down the stairs to wash the dishes. The house was quiet. But my soul wasn't.

I glanced at the worn leather couches in our living room. With each scar and scrape, there is a testament to their journey. We got them at floor price from a store in town—a bargain, the salesman had said. But there was no hiding the imperfections; the scratches ran deep, and the wear was plain as day.

Just like that leather, our hearts bear marks—visible or not—of every offense and every pain. I said to myself, "The gift of forgiveness can't even come close to the trespass. The gift of God's grace far outdoes and outweighs it all—every sin, every hurt, every picked-up offense, the righteous and unrighteous anger." The gift has always been better, softer, sweeter. I've had access to this gift, this love, the whole time. The gift of grace I had received and was called to give back was not like the trespass.

For years, I viewed forgiveness as a checkbox, a onetime decision. Years ago, I would have confidently told you that I had mastered the art of forgiveness. I would have proudly, perhaps even smugly, offered the perfect answers on how to turn the other cheek, protect my peace, or let go of the past and never look back. I might have insisted that, once I chose to forgive, that was the end of it for me—it didn't trouble me anymore or even cross my mind again.

But looking back, I now realize that my version of forgiveness often served me more than it served the healing process. I might have told myself I had forgiven, but I was really just burying the hurt—pushing it down, pretending it didn't affect me, and sweeping it under the rug. I'd forgive in a way that was more about avoiding the discomfort than truly letting go. It all seemed black-and-white, with little room for gray. I knew the right answers, but it wasn't until I faced the pain head-on that I began to understand the true depth of forgiveness, both for myself and for others.

We can't truly move forward until we confront and heal from our past hurts. And time alone won't heal these wounds, but time with God can.

It wasn't until I sat with the discomfort, felt the sting of every hurt I wanted to bury, that I realized something profound: Forgiveness isn't about forgetting. It's about acknowledging the scars and allowing them to heal properly. It's not about pretending the mark isn't there. It's about letting it be transformed into something more. This took me choosing to trust God, sit with Him, and be loved by Him. It took a small step of courage toward intimacy and surrendering all the weight that was heavily weighing on me. I had to be honest with my pain and open to grief.

Before you close this book and say, "I can't forgive them—I've tried," hear this, friend: The life you're yearning for is on the other side of forgiveness. It's on the other side of releasing the offense, where you can live fully, securely, accepted, and free from the hold that bitterness has on you. I'll tell you I have felt the disdain of having to choose forgiveness again and again—I've felt tired of even having to think about it. It's not something I've loved doing, and I had to learn that forgiveness, giving this gift, was not only to extend grace to those who wounded me but to release me from their grip too. Forgiveness isn't just for them—it's God's gift of freedom to you.

If we don't allow God to heal our wounds, the pain lingers. Bitterness seeps in like an unseen toxin, quietly poisoning everything it touches.

I thought holding a grudge would punish the person who hurt me, but it ended up punishing me instead. Unforgiveness works the same way (Heb. 12:15). When we ignore the pain others have caused, the consequences are inevitable. They show up one way or another, like a check engine light, signaling that our hearts need maintenance.

When we refuse to forgive, we become passive, cold, stuck, and stagnant in life and faith. We grow critical, walk in pride, live defensively and in fear, and hold on to suspicion. I know this all too well because I lived that way for far too long. The bitterness, resentment, and unforgiveness I carried wove itself into every day, into every conversation, and tainted the way I saw the world. My past painted my future with the same dark hues.

Hurt leaves a mark, and unless we allow God to breathe new life over the wound—unless we not only become aware of the pain but are willing to walk through it—that mark becomes a scar that never quite fades. Bitterness had consumed me in ways I hadn't realized. And when the wounds cut too deep, healing wasn't easy. This journey of learning to move past offense led me to places in my heart that I didn't know needed tending.

Nothing else matters if we can't get this part right. So much of my unforgiveness came from being hurt by people I thought should have loved and protected me. They had let me down, and it devastated me. When I think back to little Alexandra and her dad, I see so many of the same patterns of how I learned to deal with offense, or rather, how it dealt with me. I lived defensively and defeated, always trying to keep a smile on my face and keep it together with performance and grit, fighting to protect my mom and myself.

Forgiveness is often touted as a simple choice or a matter of willpower. Yet, as I delved deeper into the journey of healing,

I discovered that moving past offense is far more complex. It means living from a place of deep acceptance and forgiveness with God. It is a decision to release the grip of resentment, bitterness, and anger toward someone who has hurt or wronged us by releasing them from our condemnation. God's not keeping score, so we won't either.

Something I learned from Jesus concerning forgiveness is that it is never meant to be a pass for wrongdoing but rather an invitation to move past the wrongs into a fuller life with Him. Forgiveness gives us eyes to see our shortcomings and our desperate need for God and His grace. It helps us humbly submit to a perfect God who has never done wrong. Forgiveness shows us a grace we could never show ourselves or each other without Christ.

He meets us where we are and makes room for our brokenness and pain, our shortcomings and shortfalls. He doesn't look away but leans in. God's forgiveness is deeply connected to His ability to see us fully. He knows us inside and out—our weaknesses, our failures, and the depths of our pain. Yet His sight doesn't lead to condemnation; it leads to compassion. Like a father who sees his child's struggles and still runs to embrace his child, God sees us and chooses to forgive! His forgiveness flows from a love that sees beyond the offense to the heart longing for grace.

Forgiveness was never meant to be a hall pass for pain or sin but rather the doorway to freedom and healing from them.

The Gift Is Not Like the Trespass

Have you ever received a gift that overshadowed everything else going on in your life? Something so unexpected, so undeserved, that it shifted your entire perspective? Paul's words in Romans 5:15–17 create this picture for us of a gift given to those who have sinned. Instead of condemnation, they receive redemption. God's gift of grace doesn't just level the playing field; it completely transforms it. Where sin brought separation, God's gift brings life and reconciliation, far beyond what any of us could have imagined or earned. It wasn't a simple gesture but a flood of grace that overwhelmed every piece of brokenness in our lives. Romans 5:15–17 says,

> The gift is not like the trespass. For if by the one man's trespass the many died, how much more have the grace of God and the gift which comes through the grace of the one man Jesus Christ overflowed to the many. And the gift is not like the one man's sin, because from one sin came the judgment, resulting in condemnation, but from many trespasses came the gift, resulting in justification. If by the one man's trespass, death reigned through that one man, how much more will those who receive the overflow of grace and the gift of righteousness reign in life through the one man, Jesus Christ.

When we allow God's Word to wash over us and confront the offense we've carried and the traps we're stuck in, His truth becomes honey on our lips, a balm that softens the hard places in our souls. We begin to move from stuck to free, from bound to boundless. Grace abounds. Love abounds. His life, death, and resurrection have set us free.

But what do we do with unforgiveness? If we recognize we're carrying this weight—toward others or even toward God—how do we begin to let it go? How do we truly forgive and step into the freedom He's already won for us?

What Is Forgiveness?

Forgiveness is the act of tearing down the walls we've built, releasing ourselves from the captivity of offense, and stepping into the open space of grace and healing. Remember when we talked about pride? Pride keeps us from growing. The wall between us and the future of our lives is not admitting our need for forgiveness. To take it a step further, to admit and not act is to have not only pride but a lack of wisdom and obedience. We know the truth but are unwilling to act on it.

In Scripture, we see forgiveness talked about tirelessly—mainly, in God's forgiveness and love toward us. Here are a few verses to anchor us in His example of forgiveness:

> The LORD is compassionate and gracious, slow to anger, abounding in love. He will not always accuse, nor will he harbor his anger forever; he does not treat us as our sins deserve or repay us according to our iniquities. For as high as the heavens are above the earth, so great is his love for those who fear him; as far as the east is from the west, so far has he removed our transgressions from us. (Ps. 103:8–12 NIV)

> Bearing with one another and, if one has a complaint against another, forgiving each other; as the Lord has forgiven you, so you also must forgive. (Col. 3:13 ESV)

> If we confess our sins, he is faithful and righteous to forgive us our sins and to cleanse us from all unrighteousness. (1 John 1:9)

Forgiveness is the gift we receive from God to be redeemed from our sins, reconciled to Him, and wiped clean of all impurities because of Christ's life, death, and resurrection. It tore the veil, bringing us near to God, and made room for us to be given new life in Christ. It is both undeserved and transformative, reshaping our relationships with God and each other. We are called to forgive because of the wild forgiveness Christ gave us. Yet, as Matthew Henry says, "Though we live wholly on mercy and forgiveness, we are backward to forgive the offences of our brethren."[1]

We are called to live from a posture of forgiveness because we are living from a place of forgiveness. When we live loved and forgiven, we are empowered to love, forgive, and walk confidently in Christ's strength. It may not come naturally at first, but as we deny our flesh and its power, we make space for Christ's power to reign in us. The more we become aware of the real fight we're in, the more we realize we don't have time to waste. I refuse to let the enemy steal my focus with anger or the pain of past narratives when God is calling me to a future with Him.

I'll Forgive Only Once

What I know to be true about our hearts, especially mine, is that they become fatigued from feeling like all we do is forgive. We turn the other cheek. We're trying to walk in humility. We're trying to be the bigger person. We heard someone slight us and chose to overlook it, but it went home with us.

---

1. Matthew Henry, "Matthew 18 Bible Commentary," Christianity.com, accessed May 13, 2025, https://www.christianity.com/bible/commentary/matthew-henry-concise/matthew/18.

Our friend decided to gossip about us, and we heard about it. Now we're unsure of what to do with that information, and it's lingering. Maybe our family members don't seem to understand us, or our spouse keeps offending us with the same point of contention no matter the conversations, and it all feels hopeless.

God feels far off. We feel thin, taken advantage of, and empty. Yet we offer up a version of forgiveness. We move on, or at least try to. Based on our understanding of forgiveness, it might be more accurate to say that we attempt to forgive, but what we often do is suppress our feelings, push them aside, or manage them superficially. True forgiveness isn't just about moving on; it's about deeply releasing the hurt and finding healing with God. Even more so, it involves releasing that person to God.

I love and appreciate Peter's conversation with Jesus in Matthew 18. Jesus is coming out of His teaching on church discipline, and Peter is asking all the questions a person would ask when they want some clarity and guardrails around a sticky topic.

Some of Jesus' disciples apparently had the same problem we do—Peter was seriously confused and offended about why he should forgive those who had offended him! He asked Jesus if he should forgive someone as many as seven times. Jesus replied, "I tell you, not seven times, but seventy-seven times" (Matt. 18:22 NIV). Infinite forgiveness—over and over.

When Jesus told us to forgive without limits, I do believe He meant it. Why? Because we're called to treat others the same way God treats us. We owe God a debt we could never repay—our sin created a gap we couldn't close. In His grace, God forgave us anyway, not because we earned it but because of His overwhelming love and mercy. We're deeply indebted to Him and even more loved by Him.

Jesus knows the worst of our shortcomings—the things we wouldn't dare share with the world, the things that cause us shame and that the enemy has tried to use to keep us from seeking forgiveness and healing. Jesus knows our pain points and our weaknesses, so once we've truly experienced His forgiveness, it changes how we approach others. It softens our hearts and our ability to hold offense and to hold others hostage. They may not deserve forgiveness, but we didn't either when God forgave us. The grace we have received is the grace we are called to give. And how we receive forgiveness is how we will also forgive.

I have learned from my pain that forgiveness must be about receiving before giving. The more freely I receive Christ's forgiveness for me, the more His love flows through me. This is how His love works and how grace moves—like a river down a mountainside, rushing past every obstacle, unstoppable in its course. Easier said than done, though.

For me, the greatest struggle with forgiveness was wondering where it left my value and safety. If I forgave, if I let go of the offense, what did that mean for me? How would I protect myself?

What I've learned is that unforgiveness isn't a shield but a weapon that harms our souls. When we hold on to offense and unforgiveness, we're not protecting ourselves; we're tethering ourselves to a painful story we keep replaying.

Choosing to forgive doesn't leave us unarmed or weak. It's the most powerful choice we can make in moving forward from our wounds. Forgiveness is the release of both the pain and the person into God's good and gracious hands. It doesn't make us passive or vulnerable; it frees us to heal.

We don't have to keep overextending ourselves to people who have wounded us or can't be trusted to love us well. Until trust is rebuilt—if it ever is—we forgive, because forgiveness isn't about their inability to love us well; it's about choosing to love them in spite of it. We can forgive deeply, love with healthy boundaries, and no longer live under the weight of someone's actions. We can forgive and decide that, if a relationship continues to be toxic, we don't have to keep it. We can move forward with clarity and confidence, trusting in God's guidance to help us move in health—choosing healing, not harm.

Forgiveness, then, is not just an act; it's a way of being. It's living from a place of love so profound, so undeserved, that it spills over and touches everyone around us. It's about letting God's grace flow through us like an unending stream, breaking down walls, softening hardened hearts, and bringing life wherever it goes.

It's okay if you're tired right now. If this whole thing sounds exhausting, stop and take a breath. Your pain is not only valid but taken into account. This matters. It matters to know that when Jesus carried His cross—when He walked a path that should have taken only ten minutes but ended up being hours of harrowing pain—your pain was with Him, your wounds were with Him, you were on His mind, you were on His heart.

Caged In

I have a complicated relationship with the zoo. I know, stay with me. I both love it and hate it. As a little girl, I would visit the Smithsonian National Zoo in Washington, DC. It's a beautiful place. The landscaping is meticulously cared for, and the attention to detail is impressive. The sidewalks are lined with mist machines that offer a refreshing break from the scorching sun. There are bubbles and music, and on the warmest days, there's still a sense of joy that permeates the air—even among the grumpy parents (which sometimes includes me) who are eager to head home.

Every few years, we take our kids to the zoo, hoping to re-create the joy I remember from my own childhood visits. But each time, I'm met with a familiar feeling of guilt. I can't help but feel this overwhelming urge to set all the animals free. It sounds a little ridiculous, but I'm serious. As a kid, I would beg my mom to let us take some animals home, and I would cry at the thought of how lonely and trapped they must feel in those cages. I knew it wasn't realistic to imagine lions, elephants, and pandas roaming around freely, but it never sat right with me that they were confined in places they didn't belong. My mom would reassure me that the animals were safe, cared for, and even loved, but none of that mattered because all I could see were animals locked in cages, and it broke my heart. I think the idea of cages did something to me; it shook something up inside of me. The animals weren't supposed to be there, caged up like that.

When we don't forgive, we become those caged animals—meant to live freely but trapped within the walls of our own resentment. Just as zoo animals are confined and unable to roam as far as they were created to, we too find ourselves limited when we hold on to grudges. Our hearts are fenced in by anger, bitterness, and resentment, which restricts us from experiencing the full life of freedom, peace, and joy that forgiveness can bring. The longer we stay in this cage of unforgiveness, the more it becomes our reality, just like an animal that begins to forget what it means to run wild and free.

I felt caged in for years—caged in by unforgiveness, by people's perceptions of me, by the gossip I'd heard my friend whisper behind my back, and by the rejection from people I had looked up to for years of my life. I did not understand it.

But we don't need to understand to forgive. *We choose to forgive.* We forgive because the weight of unforgiveness is killing us more than the offense itself. We might think holding offense legitimizes our pain, but it only traps us.

When we are young, we are taught to apologize and accept apologies in return. We've been told our whole lives to forgive, but we aren't exactly taught how. We aren't sure where to place the hurt or blame, so it sticks with us. We know how to talk about the idea of forgiveness, but we learn how to actually do it only when we have to.

Satan's Trap

The enemy acts like an enemy. He's not here to play nice with our souls or lives—he's got one job and it's to kill, steal, and destroy. He wants to cause division, distortion, and discouragement. He wants to derail us from our calling and create disdain between us, God, and God's people. When we lose sight of the enemy's tricks and traps, we play into them.

I've taken my anger out on people too many times. I've walked right into situations that have not been God's best for me out of offense and woundedness. I've said things out of spite, yelled, held back love. I've seen the enemy spin such webs of lies that I couldn't tell the truth from the lies. He is a liar, a deceiver, and our true enemy (John 8:44).

These days, whenever I find myself in the middle of chaos, whether it's with family, friends, work, or ministry, I do my best to take a step back and ask God, "What's the enemy trying to do here, and how am I playing a part?" And when I've asked, the Spirit has shown me every time where my lack of humility, gentleness, compassion, long-suffering, peace, honesty, and so on has played a role in the enemy's scheme to do what he came to do—keep us separate from God and distant from people.

Jesus knew this, and He called Himself higher—out of the enemy's mud and into a kingdom perspective—when He was confronted with hurt and offense. Discerning good from evil, right from wrong, He saw past the person and spoke the sin.

We don't wrestle with people—our fight isn't against them. Rather, it's "against the rulers, against the authorities, against the powers of this dark world and against the spiritual forces of evil" (Eph. 6:12 NIV). The real danger comes when we shift our focus from the true enemy of our souls to each other, turning those we are called to love into adversaries. And the truth is, we all end up here, on both sides, both needing to be forgiven. Needing to let go and be let go of. Sometimes we are the ones people are healing from, while we are also healing from them.

In our pain and sometimes our ignorance, we inadvertently expose each other's wounds. With our words and actions, we brush up against those who have already begun to heal, wounding them while we are also healing. The only right response to this is grace—grace for ourselves to move on from that moment and continue to heal, grace for them as they heal with God, grace for the journey, and grace for the boundaries. We respond in grace not for them but for us—not to forget what they have done or what we have done but so we can take in God's grace and gentleness.

Grace is beautiful and can still be boundaried. It is not an abuse of power but a kingdom framework for how to love. We don't excuse others' atrocities toward us or overlook the need for healthy boundaries; we simply remember that we are at war not with each other but with the enemy of our souls. Abundant life is here, and we can live out freedom with God while we let go of the world of hurt we've been living in—without defeat or scarcity, knowing how to move through and around offense. This is how we move forward, knowing what we are healing from, who we are forgiving, and for what. God knows how to help us move through our hurt and pain without us perpetuating a cycle of offense in our lives.

Jesus' Way Through

Jesus' life was marked by betrayal and offense. His closest friends turned their backs on Him. He was persecuted, misunderstood, mocked, and mistreated by the very people He came to serve. Maybe you can relate. I know I can. The last few years have been filled with pain from people I thought were friends, only to watch them slip away. Some of those friendships are now just distant memories.

This kind of hurt cuts deep. It exposes the cracks in us, revealing how desperately we need new boundaries for our hearts and minds.

It's impossible to love and forgive the way we're meant to without Jesus. We can't move forward or forgive in our own strength; we can't let go on our own. But in Him, we have the power to move through the pain of life that leaves us breathless. Jesus shows us how. He gave love freely, letting His Father's love flow through Him, even as He faced betrayal, rejection, and unimaginable pain. Jesus trusted His Father. He knew how to live from a place of acceptance, whether He was offended, betrayed, rejected, humiliated, or tortured. Love kept Him going. Love held Him. Love truly conquers all (1 Cor. 13:1–3).

I often ask myself, "Am I living from Christ's love?" It's a question that brings me back when I've started to lose sight of my security and confidence in Him. When the sting of rejection creeps in, when I start to feel less than or not enough, when bitterness threatens to take root, or when I wonder if God has overlooked me, that is when I realize I've lost my way.

We Become What We Do Not Heal

We become what we do not heal. Every root of offense we hold on to only deepens the darkness in our hearts, hindering our growth and pulling us further from healing, growing, and God. But grace has a long runway for forgiveness. On this path, we can forgive others and ourselves. We learn to hold space for the complexities of life, letting go of the need for every wrong to be explained or reconciled. We come to understand that forgiveness, healing, and grace are all part of a bigger process that only God can lead us through.

Through Jesus, we become women who see life clearly, with eyes wide open to both the beauty and the brokenness. We learn to keep the enemy in his place, walk through healing with God, navigate the complexities of relationships, and most importantly, let God be God. As we abide in Christ, we are transformed to look more like Him, reflecting His love and light to a hurting world. Even the broken pieces of our lives, when surrendered and connected to Him, are woven into a masterpiece more beautiful than we ever imagined. Forgiveness looks like love—flowing like a stream, not forced but intentional. It overflows naturally. Forgiveness is not about trying harder; it's about releasing.

Let me be clear: Letting go of offense doesn't mean we ignore sin. Paul makes it clear in his letter to the Romans that forgiveness isn't a free pass for sin to continue. "What should we say then? Should we continue in sin so that grace may multiply? Absolutely not! How can we who died to sin still live in it?" (Rom. 6:1–2).

Rather than ignoring sin, forgiveness can be an invitation to set healthy boundaries—physically, emotionally, and spiritually—because all relationships need boundaries. Not everyone in our lives is helping us become who God is calling us to be. Some people are working against that. We can forgive without necessarily giving them the key to our house. We'll just see them on the sidewalk and wave hello, if that's the access they need to now have.

Forgiving and Letting Go

When we choose to forgive, what we're saying is that we love that person enough in Christ to let go of the offense that has held us hostage, and that we are willing to forgive regardless of their response. Even if we never get an apology. Even if they never change. Even if that relationship is always broken. We are still choosing to let go of the anger, the hurt, and the offense in our own hearts, which is all we can control.

Forgiveness says, "I love Christ more than you and me, and because I do, I forgive as He's forgiven us. I choose daily to lay down my anger, my resentment, my hard heart, my bitterness, and whatever other trap has become a stronghold in my life. I forgive you because I have been forgiven for sins and blemishes, for my imperfections and indiscretions. I release you to the only One who can restore you and bring reconciliation to your soul. I am not God. I am not a judge or jury—and what good news that is. I forgive you because love is the greatest command, and holding on to unforgiveness is choosing to hold back the very thing we were made to give (Mark 12:30–31)."

There isn't a bow to tie on forgiveness—it's nuanced, and most of the murkiness we have to walk through comes from our own wounds and pain with people. We must forgive the people who have wronged us and forgive ourselves for the wrongs we have done. It's a process. Pain makes its way through our minds and souls, but with God, healing can as well. Forgiveness may seem like an option, but it's really a command and an invitation to abundant life. It frees us from a life of pride, which often lies at the root of how easily we take up and hold on to offense.

Choose forgiveness. Choose to see past the offense others cause and look at their wounded soul. Choose to see them as someone in desperate need of God, just like me and you.

As we forgive, we begin to release the weight we've been carrying—the invisible debt of offense that lingers long after the hurt. In forgiving, we undo years of pain, and we prepare ourselves for the hurts that will inevitably come our way.

This is sacred work, my friend. You've walked a road no one else truly knows—a journey only you and God fully understand. When you choose to forgive, He sees you. He knows the inner tension that comes with actively choosing to forgive someone who has hurt you.

The way forward isn't found in doubling down on our hurt; it's in rising above it. To truly walk in freedom, we must understand that Jesus has already settled the debt—both for us and for those who have wronged us.

10

Leave the Burden Behind

I love stories. I see our lives, believe it or not, as scenes in a movie or seasons of a television show: season 1, season 2, season 3, each one playing a crucial role in getting us to where we need to go.

Every good story has a moment when the main character is at a crossroads, where they face a pivotal choice: How will they move forward into the next season? Will they stay stuck in the familiar, or will they step boldly into the unknown? They reach this point tired, worn down, and depleted by the story they have already survived. They've made mistakes, questioned their purpose, and wondered about their future. They're unsure of what comes next, but they know something has to change. It's the moment when they have to decide what kind of life they want to live.

Here you are, at that same moment. I know I can't be the only one dancing between the hope of what could be and the fear of what might come, longing for life to bring more healing than hurt. I wish I could show you what's ahead, but what I do know is that there is a way forward.

Picture this: You're sitting on a park bench, maybe at your favorite beach or in Central Park. You're crying, but this time, the tears are not just from pain. They are tears of relief from finally seeing what's been holding you back. You've seen the trap. You've felt the weeds that have entangled your heart for too long. You know the people who have held you hostage in your heart, you know the words that have tried to steal your light, and you know the moment it all happened—you can trace exactly how you arrived here, at this point. You can see how your skin rises up every time you see an old friend who betrayed you, or you run into that woman from church who made you feel small, or you hear from that friend who ghosted you, or you have to face that family member who seems to continually misunderstand you.

You see the hurt, and instead of trying to settle the debt somehow, you exhale. At this moment, something shifts. You're grieving and healing all at once, wrestling with God, and bringing Him every broken piece of yourself. But here's the difference: You're content. You're more secure in Him. You're more clear about who you are and who you're called to be in Him. You're not living *for* love anymore, friend. You're living *from* it.

You realize that this is what abundance feels like—not perfection but movement forward. You're not staying stuck anymore. You're taking back the authority God has given you to live as a loved woman, a forgiven woman. Your heart, once heavy with burdens, is waking up again. You're afraid, but you're ready. And more than anything, you're filled with hope for the future.

Because today—*today*—is the day you leave your burdens behind. You exhale and let it all go. The old wounds, the new ones, and even the ones that haven't been inflicted yet. Why? Because God remains with you, and in Him, you are safe. You are free. And this is what it means to live unburdened—to live loved, to live free, and *to let go*.

Settling the Debt

I want to be tender enough to say that the wounds may still hurt. They will sometimes sting when you don't want them to. I know because mine have, and still do. You see the faces you miss—the ones you've had to draw boundaries for. Anger rises in your throat because justice hasn't been served. Your side of the story hasn't been told. No one really knows the truth. And still, you've chosen to forgive. To move on. To let go, and let it be with God. Grappling with the unanswered questions and feeling the ache that doesn't easily fade are all part of the journey.

We get into trouble when we try to handle the crossroads in our journey on our own terms. Our approach often looks like choosing power over humility, defense over compassion, control over grace, resentment over forgiveness, and striving over surrender. The problem is, our terms often create distance from the healing we need. They keep us stuck in a cycle of protecting ourselves rather than letting Christ protect and heal us. When we handle things our own way, we forget that true freedom only comes from laying down our terms and embracing His.

I am sure I've uttered the words "I can't just let them get away with it" before, wondering how on earth I would ever get justice or some sort of peace for my aching heart. Because really, that's what we're all looking for at the end of the day: peace that surpasses understanding. Settling our own debt, getting justice for wrongs committed against us, doesn't work. It only rips open our hearts even more.

Payback never brings true peace. Gossiping about the pain doesn't resolve it, and looking for a way to get even still leaves the wound wide open. Idolizing our pain and trauma, letting them define us, doesn't lead to healing either. Holding in the pain and burden until the hurt disappears only makes us more sad, more disillusioned, and more ready to give up.

Imagine trying to pay a bill with Monopoly money. You know it won't settle the debt because the payment isn't genuine. We can't pay off a debt with counterfeit money, no matter how much we wish we could. In much the same way, we often try to resolve our pain with our own efforts, thinking that we can somehow settle the debt of offense on our own.

One of the things I looked forward to the most growing up was our occasional weekend visit to the local Fuddruckers. Looking back, I can't really vouch for how great the food actually is, but I can tell you how much I loved the burger and fries back then. I thought they had the most delicious straight-from-the-grill burgers, perfectly seasoned fries, the best double-fudge brownies, and an epic arcade. The goal? To rush through my meal and have more than enough time at the arcade. My favorite game was air hockey. I thought I was unbeatable. The problem was, I didn't always have the money to play. One day I tried using Monopoly money to trick the machines. I knew it wasn't real but hoped maybe the machine wouldn't notice. Not my proudest moment, but you have to admit, it was pretty clever.

Our human efforts don't settle our debts any more than Monopoly money settles a bill. We spend so much time trying to heal our wounds and settle our debts without Jesus, using counterfeit love, counterfeit strength, and counterfeit effort. But none of it leads to the peace and healing we long for. Only the love of Jesus can heal the offense that is currently weighing down our hearts. No matter how hard we strive or how deeply we work, we can't settle the wrongs others have committed against us or pay the debt for our own sins on our terms. It doesn't work that way. It was never meant to.

Think about it in actual terms of a debt. We carry around an invisible balance, and the more offense we hold on to, the more we demand from the world, from others, and from ourselves, like we're dragging an invisible burden through life. We walk around with a chip on our shoulder, hoping that someone or something will lift it off for us. But here's the profound truth that will set our hearts free—Jesus has already settled our debt. The debt of our sins, our pain, our past, and our future. And He has also settled the debt of those who have wounded us.

When we learn to live from love instead of from our wounds, we begin to experience true abundant life and freedom and forgiveness in Christ. What debts are we still holding on to, thinking they are ours to settle? Maybe:

- the betrayal of a friend
- rejection from a parent
- hurtful words from a spouse
- the judgment of a peer
- broken promises from a family member
- the times we weren't chosen, appreciated, or seen

Jesus has settled it all. We don't have to live under the weight of these offenses any longer. It's time to release them like chaff in the wind and live like the debt has actually been paid.

Like Mary pouring out her most expensive oil in love (John 12:1–8), we respond to God's goodness and grace with our lives. Not to settle any debts but to live in the freedom that comes from knowing the debt has already been paid. Can you see it, friend? This is the life we've been invited into: healed, whole, and alive in Christ. No more striving for acceptance or carrying burdens that aren't ours. No more seeking, no more resentment, and no more fear holding us hostage.

The work has been completed in Christ. It is finished. There is no need to strive for approval or settle debts. We can live loved. We can stop exhausting ourselves for approval and live from the mercy we've already found in the cross. When offense comes, we can remember the price Jesus paid for our sins and theirs, and we can let go. Why carry what Christ has already nailed to the cross? Why hurt with the pain God already took on for us?

Jesus is so kind, my friend. He exchanges all that's been breaking us for unexplainable joy. A faith formed while we heal our offense with God is a faith that's seen the worst and now knows the best—and His name is Jesus.

Hosea's Example

In 2019, God led me to the book of Hosea, a short yet powerful Old Testament book that forever changed my perspective. At the time, I had no idea how deeply I needed its message. Struggling with the pain of a wounded soul, I had heard sermons on Hosea before—sermons about God's unconditional love and pursuit of His people. But this time, something struck me differently. Hosea knew offense intimately, yet he showed incredible grace by forgiving a woman who rejected, betrayed, and offended him.

The historical backdrop of Hosea makes the story even more striking. God commanded him to marry Gomer, a woman who would be unfaithful, symbolizing Israel's spiritual unfaithfulness to God. Hosea's marriage wasn't just personal; it was prophetic. His relationship with Gomer mirrored how God loves His people despite their repeated betrayals. The pain Hosea felt was real, but so was the grace he showed—a grace reflecting the very heart of God, who doesn't keep score of our wrongs but invites us into forgiveness.

Hosea's story reminded me that we won't always be treated with mercy or love. We won't always have the relationships we want or hear the affirming words we long for. Yet through the book of Hosea, we see that our attempts to settle offense through retaliation, bitterness, or grudges are ultimately futile. They don't lead to healing or peace. Only God, through Jesus, can accomplish what we never could.

Jesus doesn't just settle our debt of offense; He heals us in it. As we begin to uproot the weeds of offense, whether it's the offense we feel toward others or the offense we harbor within ourselves, we begin to let go of all the debts we've carried for too long. We learn what it truly means to live as though Christ has already settled the debt, because He has. We no longer have to prove ourselves or strive to offer something apart from His grace.

This is the grace we've been searching for, even when we didn't know it. It doesn't make sense by the world's standards, but it's the grace that frees us—a grace that forgives because we've been forgiven, that knows the debt is paid, so we don't have to keep ourselves or anyone else enslaved to it. We don't have to keep tallying the wrongs or nursing old wounds. Jesus' sacrifice on the cross settled that once and for all.

I think back to when I was that little girl, hurting in the shadows of my pain. I didn't know it then, but His grace was there all along, ready to heal my heart, lift my burdens, and set me free.

So what does this mean for us today? It means the cost of staying stuck in offense is too high. We have access to move forward—we always have. Staying in that place of hurt and offense delays the healing God has already made available to us through Jesus. The longer we hold on to our pain and bitterness, the more we prevent ourselves from living freely.

The story of Hosea is a window into God's heart—a heart that chases after us in our unfaithfulness, in our offense toward Him, in our bitterness and despair, and offers us the chance to be healed and whole again. Hosea's willingness to love Gomer, even in her unfaithfulness, is a reflection of God's unwavering love for us. This is the same God who sent Jesus to settle the debt of offense so we no longer have to carry its burden. We don't have to work for acceptance or love. We don't have to strive to make others pay for the wrongs they've done or expect ourselves to be the ones to make things right. Jesus has already done that. Our only task is to lay our offenses at His feet and trust that His grace is enough.

It's Time to Let Go

How long have you held on to the offenses currently weighing down your heart? How long have you allowed the pain to delay your healing? The time has come to embrace the grace God is offering and to release the burden at the feet of Jesus and live as though the debt has been fully settled. Because it has.

The freedom you long for is found in release. Lay the offense down. Let Jesus, the One who paid the price for every wrong, be the One who sets you free.

Hosea 3:1–3 paints a vivid picture of redemption, showing that God paid the price to bring us back to Himself. Matthew 6:12 assures us that, as we forgive, our own debts are forgiven. And Colossians 2:14 declares that Christ has "canceled the charge of our legal indebtedness" (NIV), taking it all to the cross.

Embrace this reality: Jesus' sacrifice has lifted the debt from our shoulders. We are free to heal, to forgive, and to let go of the chains that once held us captive. He has ripped the weight off our shoulders. We no longer need to keep an account of wrongs or demand the restitution we know we've deserved. Instead, we're invited to live in the grace that has been freely given to us. The path forward won't be about erasing the pain instantly but acknowledging that Jesus has already taken it on Himself.

I spent too long trying to hold others accountable for things they were unwilling to admit, all while sacrificing my own well-being and growth in Christ. For years, I spun in my soul, trying to find what was wrong with me, searching for fault in everything—even in myself—over situations that really needed less of my emotion and more of my discernment to recognize that I wasn't the problem.

We don't need to carry burdens that weren't meant for us to bear.

The Cross Carried Us

In the midst of our deepest wounds and the overwhelming burden of offense, Jesus is the only answer. Thinking about His life, death, resurrection, and ascension is the way forward when it comes to dealing with our hurting hearts. He knew then and knows now how to love us through our pain. Our ultimate healing won't come from self-help books or a spiffy Instagram post. It won't be accomplished through our incredible friends talking us off the ledge or in countless therapy sessions. Those things can help. But it is through Jesus' suffering, sacrifice, and ultimate triumph that we have a path forward to humility, compassion, and healing.

Jesus' words from the cross, "Father, forgive them, because they do not know what they are doing" (Luke 23:34), encapsulate the essence of divine grace. Grace that extends far beyond our human capacity. Even as He endured the unimaginable agony of crucifixion, Jesus extended forgiveness to those who were causing Him immense pain. This act of grace was not just a fleeting moment but a powerful testament to the heart of God, a heart that forgives the unimaginable, heals the broken, and redeems even those who seem too far from grace.

Jesus' life is the ultimate example of humility and love, showing us exactly how we're meant to live. He humbled Himself to the point of death, even death on a cross (Phil. 2:8). But His resurrection from the dead? That's where the real victory happened over sin, over death, and over everything that weighs us down. No matter how heavy our burdens or how deep our offenses, there's always a way forward. Colossians 2:13–14 tells us, "When you were dead in trespasses and in the uncircumcision of your flesh, he made you alive with him and forgave us all our trespasses. He erased the certificate of debt, with its obligations, that was against us and opposed to us, and has taken it away by nailing it to the cross." Jesus didn't just pay for our sins—He tore down the walls that keep us stuck in offense and pride. It is finished, my friend. The offense? Removed. The weight? Relieved. The bitterness? Vanished. The burden? Released. The sin? Forgiven.

Reflecting on Jesus' sacrifice invites us to live with humility and compassion, not because we are naturally kind or capable but because He is. The more I let His love captivate me, the more I realize just how willing He was to forgive and how powerful His grace really is. And here's the beautiful thing: That same grace invites us to live like He did. We're called to reflect His love to a world that's hurting, offering grace to those who might not deserve it by our standards.

Jesus' grace isn't just a nice idea; it's a call to action. It's an invitation to let go of our need to get even, to release our grudges, and to forgive the way He forgave us. His grace helps us let go of pride and offense and see others through His eyes, with love and forgiveness. When we embrace His humility, we move past the hurt that holds us back, and we open ourselves up to healing, freedom, and transformation.

In the face of our pain and the offenses we endure, Jesus remains our ultimate example and guide. His life, death, and resurrection are not just mere historical events but living realities that empower us to live differently. *Take that in.* As we step into the grace He offers, we find the strength to forgive, the courage to release, and the compassion to move forward in humility and love. Jesus is, in fact, the only answer to a life full of offense—to a life free from the *power* of offense—and through Him, we are called to live out a story of redemption and grace.

The power to let go is in Jesus. He had every right to hold on to offense, to retaliate, and to demand justice. But instead, He released offense, showing the way forward for us. We will likely never face the cross, but we will face situations where we are wronged, misunderstood, and rejected. We often feel justified in holding on to hurt because of the real pain we've experienced. Our feelings of betrayal, rejection, and mistreatment are valid, but holding on to that offense keeps us deeply trapped—it's how we ended up here. Jesus' example calls us to respond differently. Now it's time to let it go.

The Cost of Choosing to Stay Stuck

When I think about forward movement in my life, I understand that there are moments when I need to slow down. These pauses—taking time to evaluate where I am, taking inventory of my soul—are not always comfortable, but they are necessary. For the sake of my spiritual, physical, and emotional well-being, I sometimes need to sit still and examine the wounds that have been left behind. Yet there's a difference between necessary reflection and getting stuck in a moment that was never meant to be permanent.

The danger of sitting too long in our pain is that it becomes comfortable. What should have been a brief pause turns into a place where we settle. Instead of a moment, it becomes a season, a chapter in our lives we were never meant to dwell in. When we choose to stay stuck in the cycle of offense, we lose sight of the forward movement that God is calling us to. And there is a cost to this. Delayed healing defers the life we long to live.

It's in these moments of being stuck that we hear the promises of God calling to us, beckoning us to move forward. The healing we desire, the peace we've prayed for, and the joy we've longed to feel are not withheld from us by God. Instead, they often wait just beyond the point where we've refused to forgive, where we've chosen to hold on to an offense.

Psalm 147:3 says, "He heals the brokenhearted and binds up their wounds" (NIV). But what happens when we refuse to let Him? What happens when we grip our pain, our pride, and our sense of justice so tightly that we don't allow Him to touch those wounds, or when we want to be right more than we want to be whole? The reality is, we will remain stuck—stuck in the past, anchored to the pain we've lived through, and unable to fully embrace the future God has for us.

When we refuse to forgive or choose to remain stuck in bitterness, we prolong our pain and we prolong our healing. We defer the very things we have prayed for, like peace, joy, and restoration. Staying stuck in offense robs us of the opportunity to walk freely into the future God has promised. We keep ourselves tethered to a past that no longer serves us, replaying old offenses in our minds instead of releasing them to the One who can heal us.

Tell me, how long have you held that offense? How many times have you replayed that hurt in your mind, believing that holding on to it might somehow keep you safer? It's time to lay those burdens down. It's time to trust that the God who heals the brokenhearted is ready and willing to heal you too. The only question is, will you let Him?

Jesus invites us into freedom, but freedom requires release. It requires placing our burdens at His feet. Forgiveness isn't a feeling; it's a decision. It's an act of surrender—a conscious choice to release the offender and the offense to God, knowing He alone is equipped.

The freedom you long for is in *letting go*. The healing you desire can't be accessed while your fists grip the hurt or replay the offense. We must lay them down. We must relax our grip.

Release to receive. Let people be wrong about you. Let them carry the perception they've chosen to create, while you walk with God and heal. While you let go.

Forgiveness isn't about the person who hurt us; it's about freeing ourselves from the chains of the past. I've learned to trust that God is the ultimate judge, that He sees and knows the depth of our pain, and that He will bring justice in His time. But our healing—our walk to freedom—is in our hands for us to pick up.

Overcoming the Fear

One of the most detrimental things I've done in my own healing journey has been denying my fears and weaknesses. I recognize how paradoxical that may sound, but it's a deeply human experience. A few chapters ago, I shared how much of my life was spent pretending that I was unaffected and that the hurt, the opinions, or the offenses of others didn't faze me. But here's the thing: Pride keeps us locked in patterns, feeding that spirit of offense and allowing it to spread. I hid my fear of not being loved, and in doing so, I walked around in constant angst, waiting for the next person to offend me. I was ready not just to receive the offense but to embody it.

These fears weren't just things I thought about. They became my beliefs, my posture, and my way of moving through life. Things like:

- the fear of being wrong
- the fear of not being loved

- the fear of confrontation
- the fear of losing control
- the fear of appearing weak
- the fear of being taken advantage of
- the fear of injustice
- the fear of being forgotten
- the fear of being rejected
- the fear of being misunderstood

These fears hold us hostage in offense, trapping us from moving forward and experiencing true freedom. They get in the way of the healing we so desperately need.

We don't have to stay stuck in the cycle of offense or let it rule our lives. We can choose to release it and receive God's goodness, walking out the kind of grace we've faithfully received. It's time to let go of the offense and embrace the freedom that comes from letting God's grace flow through us.

Leaving It Behind

Offense is always tethered to a person, place, or emotion that pulls us back to a string of memories or seasons we may not feel ready—or willing—to leave behind. Yet deep down, we know we must. For the sake of our soul. For the growth of our faith. For the well-being of our lives and the future we dream is possible.

Leaving it behind means choosing to follow God into the unknown, trusting His call to rise higher and step out of the holding pattern the enemy has used to keep us trapped. It won't be easy. It will take tears, raw honesty, and moments of wrestling to release the wrongs done to us. But the reward? It's freedom. It's growth. It's the courage to walk forward into a life of promise, unburdened by the weight of what once was.

Sometimes, letting go means quietly moving on and trusting God to handle the rest—especially when you've already done your part. Closure rarely comes from the people who wounded us. True forgiveness and acceptance often look like releasing the obsession to replay the offense or keep the hurt at the center of our lives. It's no longer about getting the last word or ensuring our version of the story is heard.

You will let go of versions of yourself that you used to know when offense ruled you, and you'll look at those versions of yourself and grieve for them, wondering how you got to this place. But you'll be so proud of yourself for the holy work you're doing of surrendering to God what only He can mend. You're doing your part in releasing the broken pieces so that He can mend them into something new. You'll let go of this version of yourself—again and again, as many times as it takes—and each time it will feel like a small death. But in that letting go, you'll be making room for new life to grow. And six months from now, you'll look up and meet a new version of yourself. She won't look exactly like the person you once were, but she'll carry the strength of surrender and the beauty of grace. You don't yet know all the details of who she'll be, but you can know this: Christ will be with her. He will have shaped her, refined her, and brought forth something new—something alive, whole, and full of His promises. She will be stronger than before, more healed and whole than today, more aware and soft, walking in God's promises and full of God's power.

It can be scary to let go of the things we've known for so long, but when we release the people, places, and things to God, we aren't choosing to give up on them. Rather, we're placing all our hope in God. Letting go is about shedding the versions of ourselves that didn't know how to live from love—the ones that clung tightly to what kept us bound. We can't carry those old versions into the future God has promised us. Those patterns, those habits, were never meant to free us, and they never will.

Tomorrow, when you wake up and your feet hit the ground, you'll choose how you want to move through this world. You'll decide whether or not you want your wounding to keep you bound. You'll choose to live loved or to live in offense. You'll choose to lay offense down or pick it back up. Knowing the kind of woman you want to be can help you see the road ahead, bright and full of hope. This is you—and me—walking in the freedom of a new life. It's a life unburdened by unhealthy habits and patterns, insecurity, unbelief, unawareness, and unforgiveness.

We will choose to live unbound—free from offense, bitterness, unforgiveness, and shame. No longer will we live from old wounds; we are ready for a new season. A season where God's power is made perfect in our weakness, where our limitations become a canvas for His glory. A season where our pride is struck down, making way for true confidence and security to be built in Christ.

We will step forward to love people fully and wholeheartedly—not out of fear or obligation but for the glory of God and the advancement of His kingdom. This is the turning point, the moment when we leave behind the weight of what was and embrace the freedom of what can be. Because living unbound isn't just a choice; it's a declaration. A declaration that the wounds no longer define us, that the offense no longer holds us captive. We are stepping into freedom, where grace flows, forgiveness reigns, and love becomes the anthem of our lives.

Your New Beginning

We'd spent the kind of Sunday that lingers in your soul—an afternoon with new friends in their dreamy, sun-soaked house. Their home felt alive, filled with the hum of laughter, the patter of little feet, and the kind of joy that spills over when kids and chaos collide. It was the kind of day you don't want to end, where time feels slower, like it's savoring the moment with you. You can smell the end of summer.

As the sun dipped low, painting the sky in hues of gold, one of our friends' littlest ones came running, a tiny hand brushing her face near the corner of her eye. A red toy car, innocent enough, had left its mark—a cut so small it almost seemed insignificant at first. But as we leaned in, we saw the depth of it. It wasn't gushing or frightening, but it was a wound nonetheless, and it needed a single stitch to heal just right.

Fortunately, one of their neighbors was an ER doctor. Help was close. Just a few minutes after a knock on the door, the kids were practically buzzing with excitement. It felt like being part of a real-life *ER* episode. They were a mix of nervous energy and curious excitement for their sister and friend, each clutching a chocolate chip cookie in one hand.

We all paced around the living room, aware that the next few moments might bring some pain and discomfort for our girl. The neighbor/doctor took her into a room, and we held our breath. It was only five minutes, but it felt like time stretched on. When she came out, there was a single stitch in her cheek—small but just what was needed. Sometimes one small stitch is all that's needed.

As we got ready to leave, she followed us out to say goodbye. I hugged her and asked how she was feeling.

"It stings—and still hurts."

I offered her a soft smile and nodded. I got it. My own wounds still stung, even after I'd done all I knew to heal them. Sometimes, even when it's just one small stitch, the pain lingers.

"I bet it does, babe. But can I tell you something? That's actually how you know it's healing. Your body is doing exactly what it's supposed to do right now. Isn't that incredible? It's telling you it's working to make things better. That's how our bodies heal. The wound might still hurt while it's healing, but one day, you'll notice it doesn't hurt as much. If it didn't hurt, I'd be worried. I'd wonder if maybe the stitch never even got put in."

Her little brown eyes tried to follow my words, absorbing them.

"The discomfort will lessen over time, I promise you. Today's the worst of it. You'll have new, better skin in just a few days. Listen, when we get a cut and apply alcohol, it stings, but we know it's the right thing to do, right? Our bodies are wired to feel that pain because it's a sign that healing is happening.

We have to work through the discomfort. Don't worry. I'm so proud of you."

She nodded, accepting my explanation. It made some sense to her—better was coming. It hurt now, and maybe it would again tomorrow, but healing was happening.

As I spoke, I caught my friend's gaze. Her eyes glazed with tears, and her voice trembled as she said, "Wow, I didn't realize I needed to hear that too." Tears threatened to spill, but she held them back.

I reached for my car door, pausing just long enough for us to share a much-needed hug. Pain is a language we all speak—and somehow, so is hope. There's something magnetic about it: a glimpse of light breaking through the dark.

"Me too, friend. Me too," I said, holding her tight.

Every adult standing there needed to hear it—and maybe, as you turn the page to this final chapter and step into your new beginning, you do too. There is life after our wounding. There is also relief in the middle of it. I wish I could tell you there is a way to avoid pain and hurt altogether, but learning to let go often involves feeling pain in the middle of the victory. It means walking forward with God, even as it hurts, knowing there's more ahead. There's new life ahead, even in the midst of our current pain. God is healing us in the middle of the storm. Our pain was never meant to hold us back, and God can use it to move us forward.

I think for most of us, this part of our journey stirs a mix of hope and angst. We want to move forward; we want to believe that God will be not only in the middle of it but also on the other side—and He will be. The catch for us is remembering that refusing to pick up offense and letting God deal with our hurt is an everyday choice. Believing that God will lessen the pain as we go on. Trusting that He will increase our hope, joy, confidence, and courage with every step forward. Life after offense prepares us for the new hurt that will inevitably come, but it also holds the power to draw out the version of ourselves that God always knew was waiting to emerge.

The Enemy's Last-Ditch Effort

There will be a very real temptation to return to the things that once hurt us—to revisit old memories, nurse old offenses, or fall back into familiar patterns and behaviors. Sometimes that pull even leads us back to people or places we were never meant to return to. The enemy's last-ditch effort will be to stir up what used to work on us, but this time, we'll be ready. We're moving forward with clarity, on the offensive, fully aware of what we're called to and where we're headed. Accepted, forgiven, forgiving, living from love and not for it. Bold and soft, courageous and confident, humble and surrendered. Offense no longer holds us—God does.

Only you and God know what your healing journey needs to look like. I believe that for my life and yours, what's kept us bound up this long has been the inability to truly walk with God in our pain, to give Him the reins where we have felt the most out of control in our hurt. But now we know He's with us. We know that picking up offense only becomes a greater stronghold. That the best version of revenge is in God's hands and not ours—even if it means He pursues and loves those who have hurt us. This is the prayer, anyway. We won't be distracted by wanting to get back. We'll really move forward in peace, taking God at His word: He does new things over and over again.

Our healing is not contingent on anyone's ability or capacity to love us fully or well. It's not up to others to keep us whole. I spent so much of my life trapped in offense, waiting for someone else to set me free—until I realized freedom was mine to walk in, not theirs to give. I thought freedom would come from a feeling, or maybe even from God handing me the courage to move beyond the people-pleasing that had become my default. What I didn't realize was that my freedom from offense wasn't in waiting; it was in letting go. It was in shifting my focus to see Jesus above everything else. In being consumed by His love for me, I finally understood that the freedom I was searching for had always been there. And in that freedom, I became burdened for others to experience the same overwhelming love that sets us free from picking up offense. It's not up to others to decide whether we forgive or not. To live from love or not. The enemy would love to keep us waiting for someone to help release us, heal us, mend us, change us, and move us into our purpose.

Each moment we choose love over offense, we reclaim our power to let go and move closer to the abundant life God desires for us. Each moment we choose to live into our full acceptance and forgiveness, a shift happens in our lives, and we go from defeated victims to victorious and purposeful women. This journey cannot be about waiting for others to act; it's about recognizing the authority we have within ourselves in Christ to rise above the pain. We can move on because God is with us, and He knows what's best and what's next. This is the way forward. Healing will come when we realize it's not dependent on others.

Will we allow our past to dictate our future, or will we embrace the freedom that comes from letting go? It is a choice for us to make, a choice for us to intentionally and consciously take inventory and account for all the offenses we've picked up and chosen to carry. Remember, letting go won't be for others; it won't be a way of justifying behaviors or allowing a lack of wisdom and boundaries to help us discern how best to move forward. Letting go is two things—learning not to pick up offense and learning to heal from it. We learn to lay down the things we can't control and wisely move through our pain with God. From slights, rejections, and disappointments to life-altering betrayals, we now see the trap and choose freedom instead.

I hope you see a life outside of the offense.

Do you know what the vision for the garden of Eden was? A place of abundance, acceptance, and intimacy with God. And now we find ourselves here, with a new way forward through our offense and into hope and healing. Jesus has made a way—a clear path—for us to lay down our burdens and live into our true identity, free from pain and offense. He invites us to heal our wounds, embrace acceptance, and forgive. As we allow Jesus to be our true north, He leads us to a life overflowing with grace, purpose, and the beauty of His unending love.

A New Way Forward

At the beginning of our journey, we found ourselves in the garden, where the weeds and vines of sin first choked the good in Adam and Eve, taking the course of humanity down an endless road of offense—offense toward God and each other. Wrapping us in weeds that have kept us bound, trapped, and stuck. Suffocating the hope and healing out of us. Taking the vision away and the purpose out of our hands. A garden that was once meant to be a place of abundance—God's power and presence in and through Adam and Eve—was now a place of defeat, full of offense.

We can trace the effects of offenses all the way back to the beginning of time. We can look at our own lives and pinpoint the pain, the moment that left us marked and different.

Offense, the trap we're breaking free from, once covered our eyes with its sneaky symptoms, invisible diseases, and overwhelming chains. It tried to keep us from living a life full of the acceptance, peace, and wild relief we've been seeking. Offense wanted to keep us from forgiving—for us and for them. It dangled the temptation of pride and vindication, promising us more on the other side of our rebellion and unwillingness to surrender. It's truly the opposite of our true north, leading us down a path full of more traps, resentment, fear, and chaos. And because of it, we've not known how to take up our space with God and the world, until now. We're taking hold of a holy confidence to show up in the world the way God calls us to—with His best for us.

We've walked this path together—the path to letting go:

1. *Make Peace with Your Past.*

    You've given yourself over to God's process of healing, allowing Him to undo the old and shape you into something new. This is where transformation begins—through trust, surrender, and faith.

2. *Break Free from Offense.*

    You've allowed God to uproot the weeds of offense, clearing the way for healing and preparing your heart to respond differently to future hurts. You're learning to rest in His love, secure, fully known, and deeply accepted by Him. Your identity is no longer in question; it's firmly rooted in who He says you are. You've reclaimed what was always yours: the truth of who you are in Christ.

3. *Move Forward with God.*

You've not only embraced the power of forgiveness but now live in the freedom it brings. No longer held back by offense, you understand the depth of being forgiven by God and how to extend that grace to others. With grace and love guiding you, you will now lead others into this same freedom. You're paying and paving forward what it means to be healed, accepted, and forgiven, helping others let go and walk in the abundant life God offers.

Love leads us where we want to go.

First Corinthians 13:3–7 is a commonly recited passage used in marriage ceremonies, and it's actually more powerful than many of us even know. It's the glue that holds this whole thing together. Christ gives us this love we embody. The gift of God's love for us was never like our trespass—it far surpassed it. His love was poured out for us. There's wisdom here. We love because Christ loved us—it's not fake or forced. After every offense in the world, we can let go and pick up love. This is kingdom math for abundant life. God balm.

> If I gave everything I have to the poor and even sacrificed my body, I could boast about it; but if I didn't love others, I would have gained nothing.
>
> Love is patient and kind. Love is not jealous or boastful or proud or rude. It does not demand its own way. It is not

irritable, and it keeps no record of being wronged. It does not rejoice about injustice but rejoices whenever the truth wins out. Love never gives up, never loses faith, is always hopeful, and endures through every circumstance. (1 Cor. 13:3–7 NLT)

The Passion translation adds some texture to this passage:

If I were to be so generous as to give away everything I owned to feed the poor, and to offer my body to be burned as a martyr, without the pure motive of love, I would gain nothing of value.

Love is large and incredibly patient. Love is gentle and consistently kind to all. It refuses to be jealous when blessing comes to someone else. Love does not brag about one's achievements nor inflate its own importance. Love does not traffic in shame and disrespect, nor selfishly seek its own honor. Love is not easily irritated or quick to take offense. Love joyfully celebrates honesty and finds no delight in what is wrong. Love is a safe place of shelter, for it never stops believing the best for others. Love never takes failure as defeat, for it never gives up. (TPT)

A Vision for Your New Life

When you look at your future, what do you see? I don't personally know you, but as a woman who's walked this journey of letting go with you, I'd like to say that there's a future of abundance and purpose ahead. Where you've been is not where you're headed. We've explored the impact of hurt and offense, acknowledging how they can distort our sense of direction and leave us feeling lost. But now it's time to focus on the horizon ahead—a horizon filled with hope, possibility, and grace. Think about the weight of the offenses you've carried.

Each one may have shaped you, but they never had the power to forever define you.

The gift is that we get to embrace the freedom that comes from choosing grace in our hurt—we get to choose the life God is giving us and calling us to. A life where we live on purpose where we are. A life where we are choosing abundant forgiveness and grace. A life where our hearts are more aware and prepared for the hurt that comes our way—rooting us, grounding us. A life that isn't happening to us, but one we are actually living in.

I want to play this out for us because I think it's important to give some handlebars for what's possible—and it really is. We've done the work to get here.

- We will be hurt by a friend or someone will leave us out, and it may sting—but we'll rise above it because we know who we are. It will be time to let some things go, and we will, in their time, with God.
- Someone in our family or online will disagree with us, because this is the world we live in—but we will choose to lead in love because we know what the kingdom calls us to be: women of wisdom and grace. We will discern where and how we show up. The enemy will not get a rise out of us.
- We will be betrayed; someone will let us down, and we will let them down—but we will not live in fear of betrayal. We will live in God's love, knowing He cares for us. Fear will not steal from us the life we're called to live. We will not be the judge and jury of others' actions—God will be.

- We will receive criticism, and it may sting—but we know who we are. We will no longer idolize the opinions or acceptance of others, thank God.
- We will choose to love others because Christ loves us. We will keep the enemy the enemy and remember that we don't wrestle against flesh and blood. We will be women of mission and purpose because offense no longer holds us.
- We will be leaders of confidence and grace—women who walk in authority because we have tasted and seen pain and we now know purpose. We know God's a healer, and we're going to live set free. We will not live for others but from God's love.

What if they don't apologize? They may not.
What if someone hurts us again? They may.
What if we start to feel fearful again and live from a place of offense? We let go, again.
Offense will not hold us back. We're ready to live our lives.

It Won't Be Just for Us

Our letting go can't be just for us. When we think about the life of Jesus and how gracefully He not only lived but also handled offense, we see something deeper. Every moment of His life was a reflection of God's heart for others. He didn't just endure offense. He transformed it. His responses to rejection, betrayal, and even death were opportunities to demonstrate God's radical love and mercy. This wasn't just for His sake; it was for the sake of everyone watching, both then and now.

We carry that same power and authority as women who have experienced healing through Christ. They are *in you*. It's not enough to be healed just for ourselves. We are called to be conduits of healing for others. Hurt people hurt people—but healed people can help heal those same wounds. Forgiven people forgive.

When we choose to release our offenses and surrender our wounds, we unlock the potential to help others do the same. We become the hands and feet—the aroma—of Christ, the gentleness we wish we would have had, the softness we prayed for, the truth in love we needed, the intention we wanted, the grace for the moment, and the words of life for the brokenness. We live in a world where brokenness and offense seem to be the norm, where defeat and criticism have become the starting place. But through Christ and by His stripes, we have the power to break that cycle. Our lives become a testimony of what's possible when we let go.

As women who know the power of letting go, we're called to take up the mantle as wounded healers, leading through our wounds, more capable of walking in the callings of our lives—in our homes, schools, work, families, and communities. We get to and can walk alongside those still struggling, showing them that there's a way through the pain. We get to demonstrate that God's grace is big enough to heal even the deepest wounds. Our healing not only is a private victory but can be a powerful public invitation for others to experience the same. This is the ripple effect of letting go.

Others will look at us and say, "Something is different about her." They'll notice a shift in how we live and how we love. A more free and confident version of us will show up—softer and bolder, less critical, and more clear. It will be Christ in us.

The freedom we experience is meant to flow outward, touching the lives of those around us. When we live as women who have embraced healing, we create an environment where others can do the same. We become the ones who can say, "I've been there. I know the pain. But I also know the healing, and I can walk with you through it." We know the North Star, and we know the way forward. We know who to follow out of the weeds. We've been under the vines before too.

Let your healing be a light for others. Don't keep it hidden or isolated. Let it be the tool that helps others find their way out of the hurt in their lives. Just as Jesus showed the heart of God through His life, we too can reflect His heart by living unoffended, healed, and empowered to help others do the same.

The Power and Purpose of Your Pain

I've heard it said before that our pain has purpose. Honestly, I'm not sure that saying has always landed well with me. It can feel like someone is trying to explain the pain away, wrapping it in a neat bow to make sense of it. But pain doesn't always make sense, at least not in the moment. When you're in the thick of it, when the weight feels unbearable, someone telling you there's a "purpose" can feel hollow. It's almost like they're minimizing the hurt, overlooking the reality of the struggle, or rushing the process of healing. Pain is not something that should be easily dismissed or explained away. Offense should not be picked up, but pain should be processed.

So I want to offer a different perspective—a deeper dive into God's power and how He handles our pain and brings purpose from it. Because of God's grace, there's a deep relief that comes in our pain, even when it feels relentless. It's not a quick fix but a soul-level comfort, where God enters our mess and walks with us. He doesn't leave us to figure it out alone. In His grace, He makes something good out of what seems bad.

He takes the pieces of broken dreams, relationships, and expectations and somehow brings beauty from them. He takes the very things meant to destroy us and turns them for good. This doesn't mean the pain wasn't real, but the story doesn't end there. God rewrites what seemed hopeless and brings purpose from our hurt.

And it's not just the pain that holds purpose—it's our experience of God in it. He's with us, sustaining us through the darkness, giving meaning to our story. The purpose isn't in the pain itself but in His power working through it. That's why every moment of offense, hurt, or loss can have purpose, because God's power is at work. In those raw moments, when we feel like we can't go on, that's where we see His power most clearly. It's not that the pain is magical or meaningful on its own, but God is in it, weaving something beautiful from it. He doesn't waste a single tear or heartache.

When we invite Him into our pain, He doesn't stand on the sidelines. He gets fully involved. He brings not just comfort but transformation. And in the midst of it, He whispers, "Watch Me take what's broken and make it whole. Watch Me turn your end into a new beginning."

This is our God. A God who doesn't shy away from pain but steps into it with us. A God who doesn't minimize our suffering but maximizes His power in it. A God who takes the very things that should have broken us and uses them to build us into something stronger, something more resilient, something more like Him.

This is the beauty of redemption: God doesn't just restore what was lost; He brings something entirely new. He doesn't just take us back to where we were before the pain; He takes us to a place we never could have reached without it. And that's the purpose—not to explain away the pain but to see God's power revealed in the midst of it.

Letting Go

We're letting go. This is it—the moment we take a deep breath with God and feel the freedom that's ahead, letting go of the hurt, the disappointment, the betrayal, the rejection. The broken heart, the slights, every offense we've carried—we're laying them down, and we're choosing to lay them down again. We trust that God can handle it all, that He's got our hearts covered. We know what to do with our hurt now. We know who to run to. We know whose we are. And we know the One who will comfort us through it all, never letting us down—not for a second.

We are women living unbound—free from offense, bitterness, unforgiveness, and shame. We're no longer held captive by disappointment or discouragement. We're stepping into our purpose, answering God's call on our lives, saying yes to more, even when fear whispers. We keep moving forward because we know God is with us, He has healed us, and He's still healing us.

We're moving forward, fully accepted, confident in our identity as daughters of the King, casting off the chains of rejection and unforgiveness. The things that once held us back are falling away. We've risen above the weeds and cut through the vines, and we're no longer stuck. One step at a time, we're walking into our new beginning, holding this truth: The offenses we once carried don't define us. God's love does. And in that love, we are free to live—unoffended, whole, and unshakable.

This new beginning is the beauty of this moment. It's not the end but the start—the start of living free from the power of offense and embracing who God has called us to be: women rooted in brave love. Our past does not bind us. We are not defined by our mistakes, nor are we held captive by the offenses we once carried like heavy chains.

Those chains? They've been broken. We're not the women we once were.

We're walking now in a strength that's not our own. We've traded our wounds for healing, our sorrow for joy, and our chains for freedom. We are no longer defined by the rejection of others but by the acceptance of the One who has loved us from the very beginning. And this new life—free from the weight of offense—isn't just about letting go. It's about rising up. It's about choosing to trust that God is the One writing our story. No offense, no pain, no betrayal can steal the future He has for us. This new life is about stepping into the truth that, yes, we were hurt, but we're not destroyed. We were broken, but we're not beyond repair. God takes the shattered pieces and creates something more beautiful than we could have ever imagined or written ourselves.

The cracks of our past become the places where His light shines through the brightest. He doesn't just restore; He re-creates, turning every wound into a place of deeper grace, every scar into a testimony of His faithfulness. We don't just see beauty from ashes; we see new life from what once seemed lifeless. It's transformation from what was broken beyond recognition. It's not just the restoration of what was lost; it's the unveiling of something greater, something only God could craft from the very ruins we thought would define us. It's redemption in its fullest form, where the ashes don't just fade away—they become the fertile soil for a new beginning, a future full of hope and promise. God restores all things so we can release them to Him.

This is your new beginning. As you walk into it, walk boldly. Walk in freedom. Walk in forgiveness. Forgive others, and then forgive again. Walk in love. Follow Jesus boldly into this new season of your life. The greatest thing about letting go is not just that you've freed your hands and heart from what was holding you back; it's that you're now open to receive every good thing God has waiting for you. And He has *so much* waiting for you.

So go ahead—you can let go. Unclench your fists. Step forward. Exhale. Let this new season be all it needs to be. And watch what God will do. He's not done, and neither are you.

ALEXANDRA HOOVER is a bestselling author, sought-after speaker, and Bible teacher who equips women to move forward with confidence, purpose, and deep trust in Jesus. Known for her powerful storytelling and spiritual depth, Alexandra weaves together theology and tenderness to help women heal from offense, reclaim their identity in Christ, and live free from the weight of approval.

Alexandra serves her local church in Charleston, South Carolina, where she leads with heart, grit, and a deep belief that God still moves through everyday obedience. She is currently pursuing a master of arts in women and theology at Northern Seminary. As a wife and mother, she treasures the beauty of life, finding joy in both the sacred and the simple.

Connect with Alexandra:

AlexandraVHoover.com

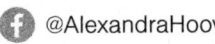 @AlexandraHoover

 @AlexandraVHoover